INSTITUTIONAL CHANGE AND RURAL INDUSTRIALIZATION IN CHINA

THE PUTTING-OUT SYSTEM IN HANDICRAFT INDUSTRY IN LATE QING AND EARLY REPUBLIC PERIOD

Peking University Series on Sociology and Anthropology

(ISSN: 2335-657X)

Series Editor: Xie Lizhong *(Peking University, China)*

Vol. 5 *Institutional Change and Rural Industrialization in China: The Putting-Out System in Handicraft Industry in Late Qing and Early Republic Period*
by Feizhou Zhou

Vol. 4 *Job Placements and Job Shifts in China: The Effects of Education, Family Background and Gender*
by Wu Lijuan

Vol. 3 *Topography of Politics in Rural China: The Story of Xiaocun*
by Zhu Xiaoyang

Vol. 2 *De-politicization of Ethnic Questions in China*
edited by Xie Lizhong

Vol. 1 *Social Suffering and Political Confession: Suku in Modern China*
by Sun Feiyu

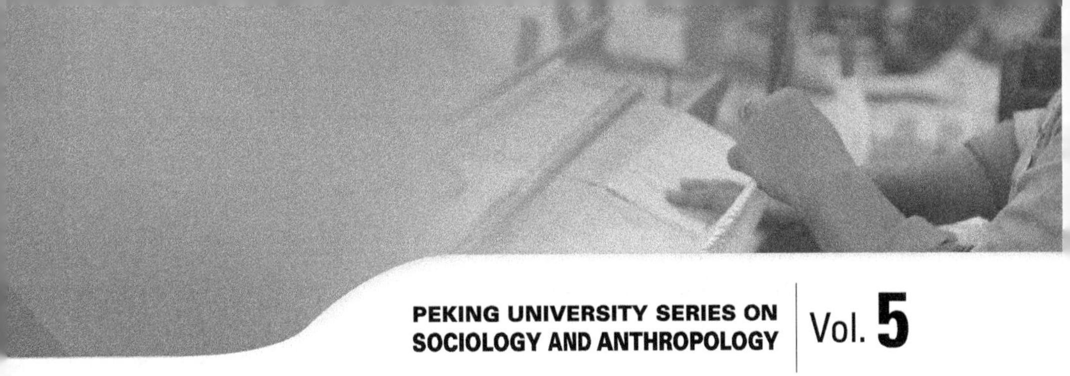

PEKING UNIVERSITY SERIES ON SOCIOLOGY AND ANTHROPOLOGY Vol. 5

INSTITUTIONAL CHANGE AND RURAL INDUSTRIALIZATION IN CHINA

THE PUTTING-OUT SYSTEM IN HANDICRAFT INDUSTRY IN LATE QING AND EARLY REPUBLIC PERIOD

Feizhou Zhou
Peking University, China

World Scientific

NEW JERSEY • LONDON • SINGAPORE • BEIJING • SHANGHAI • HONG KONG • TAIPEI • CHENNAI

Published by

World Scientific Publishing Co. Pte. Ltd.
5 Toh Tuck Link, Singapore 596224
USA office: 27 Warren Street, Suite 401-402, Hackensack, NJ 07601
UK office: 57 Shelton Street, Covent Garden, London WC2H 9HE

Library of Congress Control Number: 2018027354

British Library Cataloguing-in-Publication Data
A catalogue record for this book is available from the British Library.

Peking University Series on Sociology and Anthropology — Vol. 5
INSTITUTIONAL CHANGE AND RURAL INDUSTRIALIZATION IN CHINA
The Putting-Out System in Handicraft Industry in Late Qing and Early Republic Period

ISBN 978-981-4569-91-0

For any available supplementary material, please visit
https://www.worldscientific.com/worldscibooks/10.1142/8993#t=suppl

Desk Editor: Jiang Yulin

Typeset by Stallion Press
Email: enquiries@stallionpress.com

Contents

List of Tables

List of Figures

Chapter 1

Introduction: Smithian Growth or Involution Growth?

What are the stimuli for economic growth before industrialization? Since Adam Smith, there have been two answers to this question in economic history fields. The first one is the Smithian Growth form widely accepted by European society before the Industrial Revolution. This view, derived from Adam Smith's classic discussion, mainly refers to economic growth promoted by division of labor, regional specialization and market expansion. This mode is different from the so-called Kuznetzian Growth to a large extent, which is driven by machine production and technical changes provided by the Industrial Revolution. Before the 1960s and 1970s, economic historians generally regard the Smithian Growth form as the economic growth mode of pre-industrial societies, including non-European countries, like China, Japan, and India. However, since Clifford Geertz's pioneering study on the Southeast Asian paddy in the 1960s, more and more economists and historians have started to pay attention to another growth mode, called Involution Growth by Geertz (Geertz, 1963).

Involution Growth refers to the growth mode of economic forms with underdeveloped markets, insignificant labor division and self-sufficient, not-for-market production. The principal characteristic of this mode is that producers still insist on putting in more labor to gain growth of economic output under a situation where more input of workforce is not worthwhile when marginal remuneration starts to decline. The reason why producers do this is that it is hard for surplus labor to enter into the labor market. Geertz's findings have been applied to the research of China's economic history by other scholars. Philip Huang asserts that this involutionary situation was the most significant feature of the rural economy in China at that time in his study on North China and the Yangtze delta district. Besides the overpopulation and common occurrence of surplus labor in most underdeveloped economic systems, Huang believes that agricultural commercialization advanced by capitalist forces in the 19th and 20th centuries was one of the main factors accelerating the involutionary situation (Huang, 1986, 1990).

If one reviews the rural economy before 1949, when the People's Republic of China was founded, from the viewpoint of the two modes of economic growth, it is difficult to make judgments suddenly, because characteristics of both Smithian and Involution Growth coexist. On one hand, agriculture, commercialization of handicrafts, and market expansion developed quickly since the Ming Dynasty, and flourished under the influence of foreign economic forces during the period of the late Qing Dynasty and the early Republic of China. Besides, the trends of regional specialization and labor division were more evident. On the other hand, the agricultural productivity of many areas was so low that the majority of peasants made a living with difficulty, while large amounts of labor were put into their own farmlands. In that way, what were the main features of the rural economy at that time? How can we make a clearer judgment on the economic situation?

With the outbreak of a series of wars and settlement of unequal treaties since the Opium War, foreign industrial products were able to spread in China without hindrance by the end of the 19th century. Western scholars generally define it as a process of commercialization[1] with the fast advancement of commercial relationships and development of modern industry in China. Specifically, there are three theories on the rural economy, influenced by commercialization from the view of scholars:

1. *Recession Theory*

This is widely accepted by domestic scholars of China. They believe that the rural economy had been at a standstill or even in recession without any growth since the Opium War, and the direct cause for recession was

[1] Saying this implies that there was no commercialization before the Republic of China. However, this is questionable. In the later chapters, this study will present the development of domestic commercialization before the invasion of foreign capitalism. There is no doubt, however, that commercialization has developed rapidly since the First Opium War in 1840. Domestic production is catering to international market quickly and the internal market also has flourished since then. Therefore, I will continue to use the term "commercialization" to generalize the change of domestic economic environments.

the process of commercialization. The large import of foreign industrial goods directly led to the decline and transformation of the rural handicraft industry, to the extent that the natural economy incorporating rural farming (or agriculture) and weaving went into bankruptcy. It is worth stressing that the scholars believe that the recession of the handicraft industry directly led to the recession of the rural economy. It was hard for the farmers to sustain their original standards of living with deteriorating rural finance, which in turn made it hard to sustain agricultural investment and led to bankruptcy of the rural economy (Chen *et al.*, 1989; Qian, 1990).

2. *Stagnation Theory*

Although these scholars also take a dim view of the rural economy, they hold a different opinion from scholars of Recession Theory. These scholars investigate the reasons for stagnation of the rural economy against a broader historical background and conclude that the change in the relationship between population and land determined the general trend of economic activities. Mark Elvin believes that it was the overstocked population that stagnated the rural economy in the 19th and early 20th centuries. From Song to Qing Dynasties, both population and productivity reached their peaks, trapped in "high equilibrium" by the end of the Qing Dynasty.[2] Opportunities for business and employment provided by commercialization since the opening of coastal ports brought a glimmer of hope for agriculture to get rid of the trap. Although the rural economy of the Republic of China failed to escape from the trap ultimately, commercialization was not mainly responsibile for it (Elvin, 1973).

Corroborating Elvin, Huang also maintains that stagnation of the rural economy was caused by population pressure. However, differing from Elvin, he insists that the development of commercial agriculture brought by commercialization could not help agriculture get rid of the pressure of extremely high rations of land and labor, but led to agricultural involution instead. Huang believes that both the development of commercial agriculture and the spread of economic crops helped peasants to use their own surplus labor forces intensively, because each unit area of economic crops required more labor input. However, such intensive management was at the expense of the decline in productivity. Therefore, although yeomen succeeded in making a living by the increase of total output, the marginal labor productivity

[2]It means that profit brought by any increase of production is consumed by too many people, therefore the per capita output is hard to increase.

declined. The process of involution resulted from smallholding families taking risks to cultivate economic crops. However, due to their inability to bear the risks, they often ended up in bankruptcy, which led to the differentiation of rural society (Huang, 1985). In another book, Huang emphasizes that it was the rural industrialization that started from the 1980s that helped the rural areas to get rid of the trap of involution (Huang, 1990). His conclusions are close to the viewpoints of Recession Theory, but the logic of the statement is quite different. From his point of view, it is still "an increase [in GDP] without development" even if rural economic aggregates rise.

3. *Development Theory*

This theory is represented mainly by Western scholars. Ramon Myers and Loren Brandt are in opposition to the scholars of Recession Theory, who only attach importance to population but neglect the market. They emphasize the great influence of the commercialization process on the rural economy, especially on the labor market, in their works. Myers and Brandt point out that the commercialization process changed traditional rural economy in two aspects in spite of the heavy pressure from population.

Firstly, the production factor markets became more complete, which allowed the peasants to reorganize redundant labor and land. In other words, the surplus labor brought about by the decline of the handicraft industry in the process of commercialization were able to enter the labor market rather than be put into their own lands in the involution process as described by Huang. Secondly, commercial agriculture was booming and the cultivation of cotton and tobacco brought about by commercialization required a large amount of labor, which brought more opportunities to the labor market. In that way, the spread of commercial crops and growth of the labor market complemented each other to promote development in the rural economy (Myers, 1970; Brandt, 1987). It is worth noting that the analysis of Myers and Brandt strongly points to a trend of development in the rural economy, though they have not made any quantitative estimation of the development. In addition, Brandt has a series of articles on quantitative analysis which reveal that the income gap of peasants was not as big as the domestic scholars and Huang say, but smaller (Brandt and Sands, 1994).

Another group of scholars concentrate on the overall rate of increase in economic development. Two existing authoritative quantitative estimations on the domestic economy demonstrate that the economy developed very quickly during the period of the Republic of China but this development was only concentrated in modern industrial departments (Wu, 1947; Yeh, 1965). The latest research findings should be in the new book by Thomas

Rawski. Due to the lack of available and credible data, Rawski estimates that the annual growth rate of agriculture was between 1.4% to 1.7% during the period of the Republic of China, which is far beyond 0.8% as Yeh Kung-Chia estimates, based on the growth of per capita cotton cloth consumption and the estimated rise of real wages for unskilled workers in the agriculture and manufacturing industries (Rawski, 1989). It was even more superior to that of Japanese agriculture at that time. With a positive estimation of industrial departments, Rawski believes that China's economy had broken through the economic structure with low per capita production based on agriculture, and started to take off by the First World War.

Based on the aforementioned discussion, we cannot help but ask why scholars hold such different viewpoints on China's economic history of less than a hundred years ago that their views regarding the rural economy, under the influence of commercialization, are completely opposite. Certainly, the influence of ideology and the different methods of analysis are among the important reasons. For example, most of the domestic scholars adopt the perspective of Marxism Theory, and believe that commercialization is in fact a plundering process of the colonial economy by imperialist powers. Historians focus on population while economists focus on market impact. However, all of these are not enough to cause scholars to reach completely opposite conclusions. The author believes it is because the scholars have not reached consensus on two empirical observations — the effect of commercial agriculture and the fate of the handicraft industry.

That commercial agriculture had different impacts on the development of the rural economy is behind the divergent views of Myers and Huang. Both of them have not made estimations on the degree of agricultural development. Instead, their divergence is mainly based on the impact of commercial agriculture on the income distribution of peasants. Huang insists that social differentiation is the result of commercialization, whereas Myers maintains that the differentiation is not a fact at all (Myers, 1970; Huang, 1985). However, the key to the debate on whether the rural economy was in stagnation or at growth is the handicraft industry, which is generally neglected by scholars.[3]

[3]Neither of the authors hold optimistic attitude on the influence that the development of commercial agriculture has made on the increase of agricultural production technology and crop yields (land productivity). Taking labor productivity as an example, Huang believes that involution leads to the decrease of labor productivity; while Ma suggests that the boom of the fact markets enhances labor productivity. But neither of them have made quantitative estimation on the general development tendency of agriculture.

In studies on the development of the rural economy, the rural handicraft industry is discussed as an appendage. After careful analysis, we can find that it is the very key reason that causes scholars to reach completely different conclusions. As a matter of fact, scholars of Recession Theory, Stagnation Theory, or Development Theory all admit that there was little growth — at least in food production per capita, labor productivity, and technological innovation in traditional agricultural sectors — and that the limited growth was due to the increase of total quantity mainly brought about by the reclaimed land in northeast China. It is worth noting that the estimation of the rate of agricultural growth by the Development Theory scholar, Rawski, is actually based on the conditions of the handicraft industry. As mentioned earlier, two significant indicators employed by Rawski are cotton cloth consumption per capita and wages of unskilled workers in the rural handicraft industry, which actually reflect the growth conditions of the handicraft industry. Brandt also adopts payment of labor in the rural handicraft industry as an important indicator when evaluating the rural economy in the middle and lower areas of the Yangtze River from 1870 to 1937 (Brandt, 1989). Furthermore, scholars of Development Theory consider the increase in wages of farm workers as important evidence supporting the development of the rural economy. However, the payment of farm workers may not reflect the growth of agriculture. Even if there was no change in agriculture, the growth and decline of the handicraft industry would also influence the increase and decrease in payment of farm workers, because the agriculture and handicraft industries relied on the same farm labor. This competition for farm workers also explains why agriculture was underdeveloped, a view held by most scholars.

The main support for the Development Theory actually comes from the development of the rural handicraft industry, while support for the Stagnation Theory and Recession Theory mainly comes from agricultural production. Nevertheless, scholars generally believe that the handicraft industry faces the same destiny as the agriculture industry, either lingering on or vanishing without any trace. Therefore, in order to get a better understanding of the true features of the rural economy within the context of commercialization, the most significant yet difficult task is to understand the true features of the handicraft industry within the context of commercialization.

In retrospect, the rural handicraft industry at the end of the Qing Dynasty and the beginning of the Republic of China not only determined the features of the rural economy, but also the start of industrialization in rural areas, a development similar in importance to the impact of township businesses on rural development in the 1980s. The subsequent chapters will attempt to answer certain questions.

Firstly, did the industrialization process start from the end of the Qing Dynasty and the beginning of the Republic of China, or earlier? If earlier, how far back did it start? The main criterion that the author is using to assess rural industrialization is not the share of handicraft industry in national income; instead, the approach is to investigate the nature of the handicraft industry based on Smithian and Involution Growth. During the Ming and Qing Dynasties, most of the handicraft industries were established to meet household consumption in the natural economy, which was generally self-sufficient. Although this kind of handicraft industry accounted for a large proportion in the national economy, it had little influence on modern industrialization. However, its nature is more important for us to judge whether industrialization started or not. If the handicraft industry had existed to supplement agricultural incomes, and peasants took part in production in this industry only in the slack season (on the basis that "do or do not, one must eat; do not calculate payment, one always have gains"), the scale of the handicraft industry would never have expanded and it would have been difficult to improve its commercialization. The choice of "do or do not, one must eat" was the very reflection of the increase in involution. However, if the scale of handicraft had expanded, and its profits approximated or exceeded agricultural incomes, peasants would become workers in the handicraft industry to pursue maximum profits. In that case, economic growth would be manifested as typical Smithian Growth. In Chapters 3 and 4 of this book, the author will trace the development of and changes in the cotton textile industry during the Ming and Qing Dynasties and the Republic of China in order to establish the features of the rural handicraft industry at that time.

Secondly, historical investigations reveal that the handicraft industry had been flourishing in certain areas of China in the late Qing Dynasty and early Republic of China periods. In certain areas, almost all peasant families were engaged in cotton spinning and even the males switched from the agriculture industry to the handicraft industry, with products sold across the whole country. The handicraft industry of these periods was quite different from the traditional handicraft industry aimed at complementing the agriculture industry, and it surpassed the agriculture industry. One purpose of this book is to conduct careful investigation on these areas. What is worth stressing is that this book is not focused on the proportion of areas where the handicraft industry flourished out of the total vast areas of China, but on the fundamental change in the character of the handicraft industry. From this perspective, a more significant question is: how did this change take place? And, what was the driving force of this industrialization?

In order to answer these questions, we shall adopt the methods of quantitative and qualitative analysis to probe into the driving forces of industrialization. Besides the factors of commercialization and technical change, the author finds the organization and institutional changes of the handicraft industry, especially the emergence of the putting-out system, to be of vital importance. In Chapter 5, the author demonstrates that the emergence of the putting-out system was one of the most significant factors that led to the flourishing of the handicraft industry in a certain district, with data analysis of more than 400 counties in five provinces in North China and south of the lower reaches of the Yangtze River. In Chapter 6, the author will analyse the mechanism of the putting-out system on the handicraft industry with historical case material of certain areas.

Chapter 2

Literature Review on the Handicraft Industry and Institutional Change

The author will review what has been discussed in the Introduction and inspect the previous findings and debates to lay a foundation for future analysis. The literature review will be focused on the following questions: What were the properties and fate of the handicraft industry from the Ming and Qing Dynasties to the Republic of China, especially in the late Qing and the early Republic of China periods? Was the handicraft industry flourishing or completely destroyed under the influence of commercialization? If it developed to some extent or flourished, what was the driving force? What was the effect of institutional change on the handicraft industry?

The Myth of the Handicraft Industry's Fate

What the fate of the handicraft industry will be under the influence of commercialization is not only one of the most complicated and confusing questions in modern economic history, but also influences our judgment on the overall rural economy during the Republic of China, as seen from the review mentioned in the above paragraph.

Since the opening of China's market, the pouring in of foreign industrial products has undoubtedly had an unprecedented impact on the traditional handicraft industry. As such, what was the fate of the handicraft industry in the nearly hundred years from the Opium War to the Republic of China? Was it inevitable to head for recession?

It seems inevitable that the handicraft industry headed for recession. By the end of the 19th century, the four products that took the largest proportion in the importing commodities of China Customs were muslin, foreign cloth, kerosene and sugar, while the spinning, weaving, oil manufacturing and sugar manufacturing industries were the most significant among traditional handicraft industries.[4] Therefore, it was self-evident that foreign goods had great impact on the handicraft industry. Similar to their view on the overall rural economy, some domestic scholars agree with the Recession Theory of the handicraft industry, and their evidence is mainly based on the unequal treaties and records of customs trade. These scholars emphasize that a series of unequal treaties signed since 1840 granted the foreign commodities privileges and the control over tariff gradually fell into foreign government hands. By 1858, it was regulated that foreign commodities entering China through non-treaty ports shall only pay half of the standard duty, allowing foreign commodities to enter not only the coastal ports at a very low tariff but also inland China without hindrance (Yao, 1962). Foreign commodities had advantages of price and quality which cannot be matched by products of traditional handicraft industry in China. In addition, these privileges enhanced the competence of all kinds of foreign goods. Seen from the records of customs, soft goods, oil, sugar, metal products and paper were the major imported goods during the 50-year period from 1877–1928. Therefore, the corresponding sectors of the handicraft industry such as spinning, oil manufacturing, sugar manufacturing and paper-making were damaged heavily. Liu Kexiang and Chen Zhengping specifically list 14 handicraft industries corresponding to these imported products and reveal the degree of damage with reference to large amounts of local chronicles in their *Short Analogy of Economic History in Modern Times of China* (Liu and Chen, 1999). Among these 14 handicraft industries, the most seriously damaged and eventually destroyed was China's largest traditional handicraft industry — the manual textile industry. Since the opening of trading ports, the making of hand-woven cloth had evolved in the following stages: completely hand-made yarn produced locally; hand-made yarn as weft and muslin that is imported as warp; completely muslin. By the period of the First World War, the majority of hand-woven cloth was weaved by

[4]Silk was also important in handicraft industry, which was a little different from the mentioned ones. As there was no silk industry abroad, raw silk and silk were the most important export commodities in the 19th Century, which were "beloved ones" of commercialization. Therefore, raw silk industry was quite unique, and not representative.

machine.[5] The proportion of hand yarn in hand-woven cloth declined from 76.6% in 1894 to 27.7% in 1913 (Xu, 1988). On the one hand, muslin lowered the cost of machine production. On the other, it enjoyed the privileges granted by the unequal treaties, and therefore, it was inevitable that muslin replaced hand-woven cloth easily. In that case, even though a few sectors of the handicraft industry such as hand-woven cloth existed doggedly, it was just a flash in the pan because it was hard to avoid being replaced by industrial products ultimately.[6]

Unlike these scholars stressing the decline of the handicraft industry, some other scholars emphasize the tenacious existence of the handicraft industry. In contrast to the strong influence of the commercialization process on agriculture, Huang Zongzhi believes that the handicraft industry has not been impacted greatly by commercialization for the fact that it is not changed with commercialization as the main supplement of household production. From his perspective, a handicraftsman works for his family not for the market, as he aims to fully use the surplus labor forces and increase the general incomes of the family. Due to low cost, it can survive in certain areas amid the impact of commercialization. Huang insists that it is the most significant reason why smallholders have survived vigorously[7] (Huang, 1985). Most of the handicraft industry sectors listed by Huang belong to more traditional and special industries, like the *pitui* industries (leather legging industries) of the Lengshuigou village in northern China. He also lists the hand-spinning industries that existed in peasant households of Shanghai suburbs until the 1980s as evidence that the handicraft industry endured (Huang, 1990). Most of the handicraft industries Huang mentions are traditional but special industries, such as the leather legging industry in Shuigou County in northern China. Moreover, he also mentions that farmers in suburban areas in Shanghai worked in the hand-spinning industry in the 1980s, which is evidence for the tenacious existence of the handicraft

[5]Foreign yarn usually refers to yarn made by machine abroad. In this book, yarn made by machine includes foreign yarn as well as yarn made in China's factories. Therefore, yarn made in a factory refers to foreign yarn and domestic yarn made in factories.

[6]What should be mentioned is that domestic scholars of Recession Theory do notice that some handicraft industries were not as unsuccessful as the hand-woven industry. However, these scholars hold the views of historical materialism of Marxism. They believe that handicraft industry will surely be replaced by machine production. As a result, they do not pay much attention to the tenacious existing handicraft industry.

[7]On the one hand, Huang emphasizes the social differentiation caused by commercialization and Involution. On the other, he explains the reason why there are still large numbers of smallholders in North China.

industry. However, this viewpoint is not correct when viewed from the perspective of the whole nation. We can conclude that it is an indisputable fact that the handicraft industry declined during the Republic of China, from the statement above. In fact, the industries that survived tenaciously were the hand-weaving and oil manufacturing industries rather than the hand-spinning industry.

In the eyes of many scholars, some handicraft sectors have gained substantial growth and even reached unprecedented prosperity. Rawski revises the estimation of handicraft industry development made by Yeh Kung-Chia, and he estimates the growth rate of the handicraft industry as 1.4% from 1914 to 1936. His estimation is only limited to the cotton-weaving industry and does not cover other sectors of the handicraft industry. Although the rate was not high, however, one should note that the hand cotton textile industry thrived amid an expanding modern industry sectors which grew up to 8.1% (almost one-half was cotton textile industry). This growth rate was achieved under fierce competition with modern cotton textile industry. Furthermore, Rawski calculates the hand-spinning and hand-weaving industry together, and he finds that the hand-spinning industry was in fierce recession and negative growth. Therefore, if one calculates the hand-weaving industry separately, the growth rate shall be far more than 1.4% (Rawski, 1989). Shi Jianyun explains the developed handicraft industries, such as hand-weaving, oil manufacturing and straw hat plaiting in the North China Plain from techniques to market and organization in detail. Although without quantitative estimation, her research reveals that the rural handicraft industry did not decline or retreat negatively but headed for structural transformation and prosperity (Shi, 1995).

So far, it is revealing to note the significant difference of views on the fate of the handicraft industry. Obviously, most scholars' views on the fate of the handicraft industry are similar to their views on the development trends of rural economy. That is to say, the scholars of Recession and Stagnation Theories on the handicraft industry can be identified as scholars of the Stagnation Theory of rural economy, while scholars of Development Theory hold the view that the overall rural economy was in development. Therefore, it is obvious that the difference of views on the handicraft industry is one of the most significant reasons for debates on rural economy.

Although the scholars' views are completely opposite, one can still detect some historical facts from these debates: the handicraft industry was inevitably impacted heavily by the tides of commercialization. Under such impact, traditional handicraft sectors were divided to the extent that some sectors lacking competitiveness lagged, such as the hand-spinning industry, while other sectors that were competitive became prosperous, such as the hand-weaving industry. The reason for recession was very clear while that of prosperity was beyond all expectations, which leads to two questions.

Firstly, what was the nature of the growth in rural handicraft industry from the Ming and Qing Dynasties to the Republic of China? Was the growth achieved by farmers' inputting surplus labor forces without concerns about cost as suggested by Involution Theory or the so-called Smithian Growth achieved by division of labor and regional specialization?

In addition, how did this growth emerge and develop if such Smithian Growth existed? There are two questions here: Which areas had the conditions for industrialization? What was the relationship among industrialization and commercialization as well as institutional changes?

Stones from other hills may serve to polish jade.[8] In the literature review of the aforementioned two questions, the author will focus on scholars' study of the rural handicraft industry before the Industrial Revolution in Europe in terms of the nature, distribution and organizational system of the handicraft industry, which will be helpful for analysis of that in China.

Properties of the Handicraft Industry: Proto-industrialization and Smithian Growth

In order to fully understand the properties of growth, one shall find the standard that distinguishes Smithian Growth and Involution Growth. Involution Growth has been discussed in Chapter 1 in detail, and the author will discuss Smithian Growth in this chapter.

Some scholars believe that the economic growth from the Ming to the Qing Dynasty was Smithian Growth, similar to that of Europe and America in the same period (Feuerwerker, 1995; Wong, 1997). Contrary to that, most scholars hold the view of self-sufficient Involution Growth. One notices that those scholars holding the Smithian Growth view compare Europe before the Industrial Revolution with China, and believe that the rural industry of China is very similar to proto-industrialization of Europe.

Proto-industrialization refers to the household handicraft industry that grew widely in rural areas of Europe several centuries before the Industrial Revolution. According to this concept, the Industrial Revolution that started in Western Europe during the turn of the 18th to the 19th century

[8] Meaning "Foreign experience can be helpful in promoting understanding".

actually had a long history. In 1969, Franklin Mendels first indicated in his doctoral dissertation that the European industrialization process began long before the Industrial Revolution, and modern and factory-style machine production was just the second stage of industrialization. In his book, the first stage of industrialization refers to the flourishing rural handicraft industry in European rural areas from the 17th to 18th century before the Industrial Revolution. In order to distinguish it from the waves of industrialization brought by the Industrial Revolution, Mendels defined it as proto-industrialization (Mendels, 1969). The proto-industrialization stage refers to rural industries that grew fast and produced purely for market (Mendels, 1972).[9] This kind of rural industry spread all over Europe during the 16th to 18th century and this was the standard Smithian Growth with the following main features.

Firstly, rural household handicraft industry before the European Industrial Revolution basically produced for faraway markets, which was different from the self-sufficient mode. For example, in the rural household cotton textile industry of North England in the 17th century, cotton was imported from the south of France by merchant employers, weaved into cotton cloth and then widely sold throughout Europe. After the New World was discovered, cotton cloth was even sold outside of Europe (Lipson, 1921).

Secondly, regional specialization was quite apparent. Since the 16th century, South and North England have specialized as the producing bases of commodity grain and commercial handicraft products separately, as a result of the rapid development of agriculture in South England. The grain from the South was sold to the North, while cotton and woolen were poured into the South from the North (Jones, 1974). Mendels and other scholars believe that proto-industrialization created a market trade network of grain, which provided grain for the agricultural population that were no longer engaged in grain production. In other words, the division between industrial and agricultural areas was achieved by region (Mendels, 1972; Aldrich, 1987). This regional specialization was quite obvious all over Europe. Flax textile industry in Flanders and handicraft smelting in the south of Italy became very famous for their high specialization (Ogilvie, 1993).

Moreover, the handicraft industry led to a more distinct division of labor force. Before proto-industrialization, the household handicraft industry was basically monopolized by women. However, during the process

[9]Mendels emphasizes that proto-industrialization is for the market, which can be used to distinguish it from the rural handicraft industry.

of proto-industrialization, there were two apparent changes: first, men were engaged; second, an obvious division of labor force appeared in the handicraft industry. Taking the textile industry as an example, the mode that women focused on spinning and men on weaving became popular in Europe.

Finally, the incomes from the handicraft industry changed the social structure. The increase of income had two significant effects: first, the emergence of early marriage; second, transformation in the division of family property (Braun, 1987). The late marriage system and difficulty in dividing up family property were related to the limitation of land on population, because only one son could inherit the lands and young people without a piece of land were unable to get married earlier and start a family. As farm production was the only significant source of living, land was the guarantee to get married. However, the rural population no longer depended on land completely due to the influence of proto-industrialization, and young people working in the handicraft industry could also get married even without land. Thus, the increase of early marriage and newborn babies led to the relative surplus of population and the increase of the proportion of land and people, which ultimately decreased the wages of rural workers. It was easy for capitalists to accumulate capital and build factories to make higher profits with low wages (McCloskey, 1994). This conclusion can be confirmed by a comparative study of the industrialization process of Belgium and the Netherlands (Mokyr, 1976).

The proto-industrialization theory offers a better comparison framework for the two types of economic growth. Theoretically, it is difficult for the involutionary economy to achieve the aforementioned four goals (refer to page 14), especially the self-sufficient peasant economy. Therefore, the author will start from these four aspects when investigating the development of the handicraft industry during the Ming and Qing Dynasties. However, the situation during the late Qing and the early Republic of China was special. According to Huang's views, the involutionary growth of this period was under market expansion and regional specialization. In other words, it may be an involutionary economy even if it met the prior two conditions. However, it is certain that it was hard for the involutionary economy to give birth to a division of labor force and quick increase of income within the household. Therefore, the latter two standards will be the focus of investigation of the handicraft industry in the late Qing and the Republic of China in this book. The framework is presented in Table 2-1.

Table 2-1 Several Indicators of Economic Growth Types

Standard	Smithian Growth	Involution Growth: The Ming Dynasty to the Middle of the Qing Dynasty (around 1840 AD)	Involution Growth: The Late Qing Dynasty to the Republic of China (after 1840 AD)
Market Orientation	Y	N	Y
Regional Specialization	Y	N	Y
Division of Labor	Y	N	N
Maximization of Gains	Y	N	N

Y: up to the standard. N: not up to the standard.

In the following two chapters, the author will investigate the history of the handicraft industry from the Ming Dynasty to the Republic of China to fully understand the nature of the growth of handicraft industry with these standards.

Regional Distribution of Growth of the Handicraft Industry

In the studies of proto-industrialization in European economic history, besides the discussion of the properties of rural industrialization, another significant aspect is to confirm the determining factors for rural industrialization. In order to find these determining factors, it is vital to study the regional distribution of industrialization. Proto-industrialization in Europe was sporadically scattered before the Industrial Revolution, and many scholars pay much attention to the regional distribution of these areas. What was the factor that determined the rise of rural industry in one area without any impact on the adjacent areas?

The degree of development in local agriculture is the easiest to think of and most widely accepted by scholars. In his study on Zurich in Switzerland, Rudolf Braun finds that the villages with the most developed rural industry are located in the remote mountainous areas rather than flat areas near the city. He deduces that the crop rotation system forced the peasants to form a strong cooperation spirit, which prevents the development of handicraft industry in separated families. By contrast, peasants living scattered in mountainous areas lack this spirit and are more appropriate for developing household industry (Braun, 1966). In addition, David Levine's study on Leicestershire also demonstrates that local gentries usually prevent the presence of rural handicraft industry in areas with developed agriculture (Levine, 1977). Whether the interpretation by the two scholars is reasonable or not, the distribution rules of this rural industry by them are widely accepted by many scholars.

In the study of England's agriculture industry before the Industrial Revolution, Eric Jones points out that the development of agricultural techniques and productivity in South England promoted the development of commercial agriculture, which helped this area to be a grain exporting area, while North England with underdeveloped agriculture relied on handicraft products to exchange grain with the South (Jones, 1981). Although E. L. Jones cites Braun's unprecedented study as argument in his study of England, it is obvious that he prefers to explain the regional distribution of handicraft industry through the interpretation of economics. In Jones' eyes, the South was synonymous with subsistence agriculture, while the North was synonymous with highly developed commercial agriculture. Relatively speaking, it was easier for rural industry to root and sprout in subsistence agriculture.

Following the aforementioned two scholars, Mendels clearly points out the distribution rules of rural flax textile industry in Flanders of Western Europe in one of his papers in 1975. In Flanders, the coastal areas were populated by a small number of people, and the economy was a plantation economy mainly based on wheat, butter and dairy products. Inland areas were densely populated with narrow rural areas and its economy was based on subsistence agriculture centered on potato plantation. Obviously, the flax textile industry was centralized in inland areas rather than coastal areas. Mendels interprets that seasonal use of labor forces brought by potato plantation gave rise to the prosperity of the flax textile industry during the slack season (Mendels, 1975). In addition, he also indicates that population pressure and rural industry interact with each other (Mendels, 1972).

In the conclusion of his regional empirical study conducted in 1980, Mendels builds a model of rural industry distribution. He revises the above scholars' and his own views, and believes that it is easier for rural industry to exist in the boundary between commercial agriculture and subsistence agriculture. This is because the agricultural labor forces in subsistence agriculture areas will flow into the commercial agriculture areas seasonally in these boundaries, while they will become the best labor forces for rural industry in the slack seasons. In addition, it is easy for agricultural labor forces to flow out to the heartland of subsistence agriculture; while in the heartland of commercial agriculture, the transportation cost of merchant employers will be higher due to vast land and scattered population; the boundary is the best region to develop rural industry with both centralized population and a stable supply of labor forces (Mendels, 1980).

Some other scholars emphasize the influence of land-use rights and the inheritance rights system on rural industry. From their viewpoints, population pressure and subsistence agriculture are not exogenous factors but the result of evolution of the land system. Through his study on Suffolk, Joan Thirsk believes that the inheritance system of land division and the well-developed owner-peasant system allowed the young labor forces in that area to remain there, which resulted in early marriage and population pressure. Thus, the rural wool textile industry flourished (Thirsk, 1961). On the contrary, Mendels holds that the ubiquity of absentee landlords and the well-developed tenancy system in Flanders were some of the driving powers for rural industry (Mendels, 1975).

Although scholars try to find reasons for the development of rural industry from the economic, societal, cultural and other aspects, the aforementioned studies imply that population pressure and subsistence agriculture were significant factors that contributed to the development of rural economy, be it endogenous or exogenous factors.

Some scholars put forward different views. Empirical studies by Wolfgang Mager and Carlo Belfanti demonstrate that whether one area has natural resources as raw materials for rural industry, has decisive influence on the development of rural industry (Mager, 1993; Belfanti, 1993). Whether flax grew here determined the fate of the flax textile industry of the region. Meanwhile, whether one area owned iron mines was closely linked with the development of the iron-melting industry, and other factors seem unimportant. Gay Gullickson comes up with different views from the aforementioned scholars in her series articles on proto-industrialization. In the empirical study on one region of France, she finds that proto-industrialization only developed in areas of well-developed commercial agriculture. Her argument is clear: it was the seasonal unemployment and concentration of landholdings (the popularization of ranch) brought by commercial agriculture that resulted in proto-industrialization rather than subsistence agriculture.[10] Commercial agriculture areas needed more labor forces in the farming season, which made industrialization a pressing need

[10]Intensive labor was necessary for commercialization of crops, however, most of these increased labor inputs were focused on the farming season rather than equally distributed within a year, which enlarged the difference of demand between the farming and slack seasons. Therefore, it may have caused serious seasonal unemployment.

in the slack season. More importantly, this area required strong livestocks for deep ploughing due to the soil and natural conditions, and only large farms could meet the conditions. Thus, the concentration of landholdings and increase of landless peasants resulted in the rural industrialization there (Gullickson, 1983).

In conclusion, we can understand that it is very hard to find the determining factors through the case study method, though proto-industrialization was widespread in Europe before the Industrial Revolution. This is because most of the scholars adopted the method of case study and the conclusions from their case studies are hard to apply in other areas. For instance, Mendels claims that he has constructed a model for distribution rules of industrialization, but it is utterly useless beyond Flanders. The result of case study is just as we have revealed earlier: the same factor will have an opposite effect in another place. For example, land decentralization was deemed as helpful for the development of the rural industry in some places, while scholars find that land centralization was helpful for proto-industrialization in other places.

To solve this question, the author will conduct a trans-regional quantitative analysis in Chapter 5. With that, one is likely to find widely-applicable determining factors for proto-industrialization rather than those centering around just one region. Although the analysis is very common within other research areas, scholars have not applied it to the historical study of proto-industrialization. With the aid of the results from case studies by previous scholars, the author will develop a series of empirical research hypotheses to find out the determining factors for rural industrialization of one region and the importance of these factors in this book.

Power of the Handicraft Industry: The Putting-out System and Institutional Changes

Besides finding out the regional distribution of handicraft industry and the determining factors, one should analyze the specific effect of these factors. Why was a handicraft industry more advanced than another? How did technological and institutional factors work? Fortunately, not only foreign scholars have contributed to solving these problems but also domestic scholars have done a lot of work on reasons why some handicraft industries flourished during the end of the Qing Dynasty and early Republic of China. This part presents a related literature review.

During the late Qing Dynasty and early Republic of China, why could some handicraft industries gain such great development as industrialization went on? Of course, it is easy to understand the industries that flourished along with international trade, such as the plaited straw industry and hair-net industry, for they developed without competitors in the international market explored by foreign trade. Some traditional specialty industries, such as the New Year painting industry of Yangliuqing in Tianjin and the reed mat industry in Huantai, Shandong, however, developed rapidly in the domestic market for they experienced little impact of modern industrial products. Despite these, the most puzzling was the rapid development of some handicraft industries such as the hand-woven industry and the paper industry. They faced direct competition from foreign modern industries and domestic machine production, while handicraft products and industrial products were direct rivals. Take the hand-woven industry as an example, homespun was popular in the Yangtze River Delta and North China Plain at the turn of the 19th and 20th centuries when mass foreign cotton products poured into China and lots of domestic modern factories were established. Why did the handspun industry grow under such great pressure? The explanations are as follows.

A significant factor was customer's preference. Early foreign merchants and some Chinese scholars deemed the cheap machine-made cloth as not acceptable by numerous working classes for it was not as durable as homespun. When the price of foreign machine-made goods was the same as or even lower than that of homespun, most people still chose homespun. But this explanation cannot hold water. Firstly, it is an undeniable fact that homespun was more durable than machine-made cloth. But the homespun referred to was made by hand-spinning.

> "Short staple cotton produced in China can be made into roving only, which is equal to 16 to 20 yarns. The roving can be made into good cloth without using glue or paste. The roving made cloth is so strong and comfortable that the poor prefer it." (*Commercial Reports*, 1870–1880. See Yao, 1962)

Thus, it can be seen that the secret lies in that homespun was durable because it was made by hand-spinning. But the time when the homespun industry achieved prosperity was at the beginning of the 20th century, when hand-spinning had been abandoned for a long time and replaced by muslin yarn made in factories. Thus the view that homespun competed with machine-made cloth at that time is obviously unreasonable. Secondly, muslin was unacceptable to the Chinese in the beginning for it was too slim and fragile. When it dominated the domestic market, it was still unwelcome in many homespun industrial areas. However, the homespun produced with home-spinning as weft yarn and muslin as warp yarn could not resist the muslin's access to market in the end (Xu, 1992). Thus customer's preference alone cannot explain this problem.

Another explanation is based on technological advancement. By comparing the productivities of machine-made yarn and handicraft yarn as well as homespun and machine-made cloth, Yan Zhongping deems that the factor determining the competitive ability of homespun is technological advancement of the hand-woven industry. Productivity of machine-spinning was 40 times that of hand-spinning, but the gap was only three times that of weaving. This means that homespun could compete with machine-made cloth in the same market considering the relatively low gap in productivity (Yan, 1955). His interpretation is quite reasonable but only in part. The iron-wheel machine with foot pedal of several hand-woven industry centers in North China was used for comparing productivity, according to Yan. While slightly improved automatic shuttle looms[11] were widely used in several big weaving industries south of the Yangtze River such as Nantong, the efficiency of which was eight times lower than that of power looms. Although four times and eight times in technological difference are not big figures in the weaving industry, there was great difference in labor productivity. There must be other interpretations why handspun could compete with machine-made cloth despite their low efficiency.

A third explanation is the low cost of labor force in the homespun industry. In his book *Cotton History of China*, Zhao Gang deems that the most important reason why handspun survived under the pressure of foreign and domestic machine-made cloth was that woven households produced homespun regardless of the cost of labor force. Even though there is no quantitative evidence on the cost of labor force of the handicraft industry and machine weaving industry, Zhao insists that the cost of labor force of the homespun industry was lower than that of urban factories (Zhao and Chen, 1977). What Zhao interprets supports the conclusion of a study on rural handicraft industry in the 17th century in Europe by Levine. Levine points out that the reason why rural handicraft industry flourished and even prevailed against the urban handicraft industry led by the guilds in the 17th and 18th centuries was that there were cheaper labor forces in

[11]The most traditional weaving machine has the lowest efficiency. The shuttle machine appeared in the late Qing Dynasty. The change from "pick" to "shuttle" made it possible to have twice the speed and efficiency of the original machine. During the Republican period, the pedal machine was introduced from Japan to China; the wheel was made up of iron, so it was possible to use the wheel as the motive power instead of hand, hence the efficiency was double that of the shuttle machine (Yan, 1963).

rural areas compared with those in cities. He continues to use the concept of involution to describe the rural handicraft industry in Western Europe and also reveals the fact that peasant households pursued more income regardless of the law that marginal income decreases with more labor force input (Levine, 1977). Regardless of the rationality of his view, the object in his discussion is obviously different from that in Zhao's. In Levine's discussion, the competitor of the rural handicraft industry was the urban handicraft industry led by the guild with significant characteristics of a feudal nature, while it was foreign machine production that is believed to be the competitor of the hand-woven industry in Zhao's discussion. Even though it is generally accepted that modern industry lowered the costs of products as well as labor by improving labor productivity, quality control and other means, its labor cost, however, was not necessarily higher than that of the hand-woven industry. According to the historical fact when homespun industry achieved its peak in North China, the view of Zhao that handicraft production was conducted regardless of labor cost has insufficient statistical support in weaving areas. On the contrary, a series of historical materials show that spinning households regarded cotton textile as the main source of jobs in several famous weaving areas in North China and produced for the market entirely and their total income was approximately three times higher than that of peasant households (Peng, 1962c).

The three aforementioned views are the main interpretations on the flourishing of the hand-woven industry during the late Qing Dynasty and early Republic of China. Not only do they have inadequate evidence from historical materials, but they also pay inadequate attention to the organizational and institutional changes within the homespun industry.

In fact, despite the technological advancements such as muslin replacing handicraft yarns, underpick looms being replaced by the automatic shuttle loom and the iron-wheel machine, the homespun industry changed significantly in terms of organizations and institutions. Although the hand-woven industry reached its peak in the Ming Dynasty (1368–1644), the mode that one sold what he wove in small households changed radically until the late 19th century when foreign cotton textile products poured into China. A new production and market institution — the putting-out system — arose in cloth-weaving centers of the Yangtze River Delta and North China Plain.

The putting-out system meant that rural households got raw materials from traders and made products at home; they then gave the products to traders and gained income. This system was completely different from the traditional handicraft industry. In the traditional mode, rural households bought raw materials from the market or produced them on their own, for example, they spun cotton to use as the raw materials for weaving. They then sold the handicraft products in the market. Before the 20th century, the cotton textile industry in China was well-developed but they were all weaved and sold by the peasants themselves. Furthermore, no new organizational and producing forms emerged (Wu, 1985). The putting-out system appeared when muslin poured into the markets of China.

In the late Ming Dynasty and the early Qing Dynasty, putting-out traders were active in three cloth-weaving centers of North China — Baodi, Weixian and Gaoyang. Gaoyang has the most detailed records about putting-out traders. According to the records, there were mainly three sources for putting-out traders in Gaoyang: (1) Former cloth dealers; (2) Former businessmen engaged in other business (such as grain and grocery store); (3) Non-local traders who started to settle down there, issuing raw materials and gathering cloth. Buying muslin and textile machines from Tianjin and handing them out to peasant households, these putting-out traders gathered the cloth and then gained profit by selling them to other counties.

Putting-out traders (also called *Buxian Zhuang* in Gaoyang) have a close relation to the flourishing of the hand-woven industry in Gaoyang. Dating back to the time when Emperor Guangxu (1875–1908) was in reign, there were four cloth and spinning shops rising there. Until 1911, the first year of the Republic of China, when the hand-woven industry of Gaoyang reached prosperity, the number of cloth and spinning shops reached up to seven. With the development of the hand-woven industry, new shops were founded there every year and by 1935 the number reached 60. Besides the putting-out traders who managed the standard business of "releasing yarns and gathering cloth", there were many dyeing-line factories in Gaoyang which also operated the same business on a smaller scale.

Although records on the development of the putting-out system in other cloth-weaving areas of North China are far from adequate, the development of this system progressed along with the blossoming of the homespun industry. The synchronous relation proves that this system was closely related to the development of the homespun industry. Thus the competition between homespun and machine-made cloth was not just competition between the iron-wheel machine and the electric weaving machine, but also a contest between the putting-out system and the factory system. The result is far beyond the expectations of all economic organization theorists as well as economic historians. Until 1937, the starting year of Japan's overall invasion of China, the proportion of homespun in the total expenditure saw a slight decline even though there was no sign of decline in Nantong of Jiangsu and Weixian of Shandong in the number of weaving machines and production of homespun (Chang, 1998). Suppose that the putting-out system played a key role, the "surprise" should be interpreted with more evidence for this phenomenon in contrast to the classical organization theory from the perspective of economics. According to economic organizational theory, the putting-out system should have an irreparable disadvantage compared with the factory system and it was impossible for this system to defeat the modern factory system.

Economic historians studying the Industrial Revolution of Europe admit that the Industrial Revolution was not only a revolution of technology but also a revolution in production organization (Landes, 1997). The Industrial Revolution was also a process where the modern factory system replaced the widespread putting-out system in Europe rapidly. Although the putting-out system could compete with the urban handicraft guild system in the 16th and 17th centuries, it was completely defeated by the burgeoning modern factory system. Some scholars deem it to be the result of technological revolution that the factory system replaced the putting-out system as machine production required the concentration of production organizations in time and space (Mantoux, 1983; Landes, 1986; Jones, 1987). However, the mainstream view is that, even without technological change, factory system is innately better than putting-out system as an organizing system.

Refuting the "technological determinism" developed by Landes and others, some scholars deem the factory system built and well-developed long before the steam engine was invented. What is interesting is that cotton textile production had actually been industrialized before machines were used, which is usually regarded as evidence of "technical determinists" (Jenkins, 1975). Now that mass historical records prove that factorization had been common before the steam engine was invented, technological revolution was the result rather than the reason of organizational revolution. The reason why organizational revolution occurred was not only to meet the technological advancement but also because the factory system had advantages that the putting-out system could not match.[12]

[12]In fact, the putting-out system could also be good. Compared with the traditional guild system, the production cost of the putting-out system was low, because the production process was realized at home, and laborers had to eat on their own. Besides, women and children could work at any time. Under the unstable circumstances of trade, the putting-out system could adjust to the market by increasing or reducing laborers.

Compared with the factory system, the putting-out system had two significant weaknesses. On the one hand, dispersion of production hindered technical promotion. On the other hand, it was difficult to control production effectively (Magnusson, 1991).

Ephraim Lipson, an economic historian, indicates that in the context of the putting-out system, a wool textile household was usually employed by more than one putting-out trader simultaneously. As a result, the profit brought by the technological advancement and inventions could not be guaranteed leading to putting-out traders lacking motivation to pursue creation (Lipson, 1921). As for the factory system, internal supervision ensured the profit brought by new technology (North 1981:168). Another obvious advantage brought by factorization was that "it can combine supervisions on workers and production equipment." (Jenkins, 1975: 71) The key feature of factorization was centralization of all kinds of production resources. From the perspective of property right economics, it strengthened control of production by the redistribution of property rights. Compared with the putting-out system, the factory system internalized various kinds of resources for production. The ultimate result of internalization was effective reduction of transaction costs included in the processes of production, distribution and creation (Williamson, 1985, esp. Ch. 9). Among the transaction costs, moral hazard was seen as the mortal wound of the putting-out system. The dispersion of household production in the putting-out system made putting-out traders strong in will but weak in power about controlling the process of production (Marglin, 1974). Unlike the factory system, the putting-out system could hardly stop the occurrence of embezzlement and fraud and even encouraged these actions, including stealing part of raw materials to sell, cheating on workmanship and materials, adulteration and so on. Mass historical records reveal that these actions were common in the organizations of the putting-out system before the Industrial Revolution (Lipson, 1921; Rule, 1981; Berg, 1985). In such a context, some putting-out traders turned a blind eye to the actions mentioned earlier and even regarded such transactions as part of the pay to the workers because they were hard to stop. Maxine Berg deems that fraud had been a legal custom in some areas (Berg, 1985: 309). From the point of view of these scholars, it was hard for the putting-out system to resolve this fatal question which was a characteristic of the putting-out system. Ultimately, dispersion of production was the main reason why the putting-out system was replaced by centralized factory organizations.

As a conclusion to the comparison of the two organizational forms, Oliver Williamson lists detailed comparisons between the two systems in 11 aspects in one of his articles, such as transportation cost, stock cost, preventing fraud, etc. and finds that the factory system was superior to the putting-out system in seven aspects (Williamson, 1983). Some scholars do not agree with Williamson. For example, Steven Jones argues that the 11 aspects are different in importance and that the factory system was superior to the putting-out system in seven aspects cannot entirely explain why the factory system survived (Jones, 1982; 1983). Rick Szostak argues that the reason the factory succeeded ultimately was only because of the rapid development of transportation in Western Europe in the late 18th century (Szostak 1989). Although there is no agreed conclusion on specific factors deciding the success of the factory system, it is a fact that it has replaced the putting-out system due to great advantages.

After investigating the theories of system comparison, it is more puzzling for the flourishing of the putting-out system as well as the homespun industry. Now that the putting-out system was at a disadvantage compared with the factory system and machine production, then why did the historical facts in the late Qing Dynasty and early Republic of China conflict with the theories mentioned previously? I will explore this question in detail in Chapter 6.

Research Hypothesis and Evidence

I will study the nature of the handicraft industry dating back to the late Ming Dynasty and the early Qing Dynasty. Most of the evidence in this book are based on references and historical documents, for few statistical materials before the Republic of China can be utilized in this research. There are many more available records on development of the macro-economy, such as the prosperity of regional specialization, the commercial market as well as the exchange of commodities. However, there is little analysis about the labor force division within a family in the handicraft industry, especially in the cotton textile industry. Such micro-level studies are relatively inadequate in the field of historical economics. As for the impact of the cotton textile industry on a peasant's net income, it can only be calculated based on the existing materials and previous research. The labor force's net income is a key factor in distinguishing whether the development was Smithian or Involution Growth. This will be the main topic of Chapters 3 and 4.

The relatively abundant statistical materials during the Republic of China will contribute to the macro-level quantitative analysis. In Chapter 5, I will study regional specialization and change of the cotton textile industry to discover where the homespun industry developed well as well as the main factors influencing regional industrialization. Furthermore, I will try to answer the question by utilizing a quantitative model.

There are two important reasons why I chose county-level data to construct the model of analysis.

Firstly, the county has been the most basic administrative unit in the long history of China. Every dynasty set the rudimentary administrative organization in the county. The ecological environment, culture and customs were almost the same in one county. Moreover, the county was a basic trade market for handicraft products. Most scholars, whether Huang and Fei Xiaotong who emphasize the village as a basic research unit, or Skinner who regards the union of several villages as a research unit, pay more attention to the market scale of agricultural products rather than that of handicraft products. Peasants could directly sell agricultural products and livestock in the bazaar situated in the center of several villages. However, the handicraft products, such as cotton, paper, iron tools, and so on, needed to be sold in bigger bazaars or through agents which existed only in the bazaars near the counties. Besides, only the markets near the counties had greater purchasing power because most landlords and merchants lived in the counties. When it is said that a handicraft product was sold "in local area", it means that the product was sold within a county. If products were carried out of the county by dealers, the trade would be a kind of inter-county trade. The difference between inter-county trade and local trade would be a sign whether the handicraft industry had formed regional professionalization and distribution among various local areas in this research. Another basic criterion determining the difference is whether products were sold to markets beyond the county.

Secondly, it is very difficult to find historical materials on the household and village levels let alone construct an analytic model. Although province-level materials can be found in some statistical yearbooks compiled by the government, they cannot be used. First, the number of cases in the statistical yearbooks is too few (less than 30 provinces). Second, the situation in each province was too different to be considered as a whole. In comparison, we can find more county-level material, for there were 60 to 100 counties in one province. Moreover, we can find most statistical materials on population, land, agriculture as well as the handicraft industry at this level. Quantitative analysis based on this cannot only describe the distribution and development of the handicraft industry effectively, but also verify the previous arguments on handicraft industry during the Republic of China.

Investigation and analysis of economic organizations in the handicraft industry will be the main topic of Chapter 6. I assume that rapid changes of economic organizations played a key role when traditional handicraft industry competed with modern industry. This explanation is different from the views of scholars mentioned previously. The putting-out system that emerged in the homespun industry reorganized the household-production system and also made great progress in technology promotion, market expansion and quality control. As a result, the putting-out system not only destroyed and reorganized traditional homespun industry but also ended the competition with machine-made cloth in a draw.

Although I emphasize the importance of the putting-out system in my research, I do not mean that the putting-out system, as a kind of economic organization, was more effective than the factory system. The "exception" in economic history is usually the result of special historical tradition combined with the environment. Chapter 6 will present the institutional advantage of the putting-out system which was closely related to the special historical environment during the late Qing Dynasty and the early Republic of China. Just as the saying goes, "the times produce their heroes". I will explain the historical environment in detail, and put emphasis on the analysis of the special advantages of the putting-out system in the specific environment in which the market price fluctuated greatly with fierce competition and capital market was underdeveloped. Besides, I will also explain that the success of the homespun industry is a good example of institutional change in the special historical environment through the comparison of production and organizational patterns between the putting-out system and those of domestic cotton textile factories.

I pay much attention to the cotton textile industry when I study the changes of organizational patterns of the handicraft industry, not only because it was the most developed industry in both modern industry and handicraft industry but also because there are plentiful historical materials on cotton textile industry, which include records of employment of the homespun industry done by Wu Zhi in Hebei Province, and Fang Xianting's investigations on cotton textile industry organized by Nankai University in China's Economy Research Center (These investigations were mainly carried out in Baodi, Gaoyang of Hebei Province). As for south of the

Yangtze River, *Homespun History in the South Yangtze River* compiled by Xu Xinwu and *Homespun History of Nantong in Recent Years* composed by Lin Jubai collect a lot of original hand-woven industry materials, from which we can find out the production and organizational pattern of the cotton textile industry. I will compare quantitatively the hand-woven cloth with machine-made cloth on cost and profits with the help of these materials and related statistical yearbooks as well as specialty data in several provinces, through which I cannot only explain the handicraft industry's institutional advantages but also challenge the traditional view that the handicraft industry was only a supplement to agriculture and that the gain was roughly equal to that of agricultural products.

Research Areas and Scope

After the Opium War, the base via which Western capitalism invaded China gradually moved north from Guangdong Province. As more unequal treaties were signed and more coastal cities were forced to open for trade, the Yangtze River delta and the three provinces of Ji (Hebei Province), Lu (Shandong Province), and Yu (Henan Province) developed commerce most rapidly by the early 20th century.

Situated in the lower reaches of the Yangtze River and bearing rather good climate and geographical conditions, Su (Jiangsu Province) and Zhe (Zhejiang Province) were the most developed areas since the North Song Dynasty (960–1127) moved to the south. The irrigation system was established in agriculture, leading to substantial increase of rice's unit production. The population became larger. As the proportion of land to each person became smaller, the handicraft industry and sideline industries developed rapidly. During the Ming Dynasty and the Qing Dynasty, the most developed handicraft industries gathered here, among which the cotton textile industry in Jiangsu Province as well as the silk industry and tea-making industry in Zhejiang Province were especially famous. Since treaty ports opened, Jiangsu Province and Zhejiang Province made Shanghai their trading base, from which commodities were exported and a large number of foreign industrial products were imported. During the first half of the 19th century, a good deal of homespun produced in south Jiangsu Province was exported to the UK in large quantities, where they were regarded as the best fabric and called "Nankees". Moreover, the value of silk and tea in these two provinces ranked the first among the exports during the 19th century.

Shandong Province and Hebei Province in North China, as well as the northern part of Henan Province, have dry, windy weather and adequate sunlight which are suitable for the growth of cotton. They have grown cotton from early on and have gradually stood out as important cotton-growing areas since the Ming Dynasty and the Qing Dynasty. The cotton textile industry was not as popular as that in Jiangsu Province. Qingdao and Yantai in Shandong Province, along with Tianjin in Hebei Province, have been the only ports next to Shanghai and Guangdong since treaty ports opened. Meanwhile, railways in North China are the most intensive with Jiaoji Railroad (connecting Jinan and Qingdao), Jinhu Railroad (connecting Tianjin and Shanghai), and Pinghan Railroad (connecting Beijing and Hankou, Wuhan) running through the three provinces and leading to the Ports of Tianjin, Qingdao, and Yantai. Not only did the highly commercialized cotton and tobacco industries develop on both sides, but so did the handicraft industry along the railways change promptly under the influence of commercialization. In other words, these five provinces possess traditional handicraft industry, which was heavily influenced by their high degree of commercialization. Thus, these five provinces are the perfect areas through which problems in this paper can be investigated.

All in all, these five provinces were China's economic, political and cultural centers at that time. Among these areas, Beijing and Nanjing are famous political centers as well as historical cities; Shanghai and Qingdao are large industrial and commercial centers. The research on these five provinces in eastern China is nothing less than a research on a "mini-type China".

Chapter 3

Proto-industrialization in the Industrial Era: A Historical Study about the Cotton Textile Industry in North China

This chapter and the next one will carry out a historical study about the nature of the cotton textile industry in North China and south of the Yangtze River during the period of the Ming Dynasty, the Qing Dynasty and the Republic of China. Based on the study about primary industrialization in Europe in the last chapter, this chapter tries to answer one basic question: Were there any areas in China which formed "rural industry" or "primary industrialization" like those in Europe? In other words, were there signs of a scattered handicraft industry in rural areas being organized by remote dealers and forming handicraft concentration producing areas like Flanders and the south of Italy? Located in the east of Eurasia, China is far away from Western Europe and filled with ocean of rural economy like Western Europe before the Industrial Revolution in the 17th and 19th century, with handicraft industry scattered among the rural family's sideline. Next let us search the islands aimed at remote trade, which are surrounded by ocean of "self-sufficient" natural economy. These islands will be the starting point for me to analyze why China's handicraft industry changed rapidly in modern times. I will study the background of producing and circulating handicraft since the Ming and Qing Dynasties, and then I will analyze the two most developed areas — Hebei Province, Shandong Province and Henan Province in North China and Jiangsu Province and

Zhejiang Province[13] in the lower reaches of the Yangtze River respectively, during which I will try to make the island of primary industrialization and the island being formed clear.

Starting from Trade: Local Bazaar, Regional Market and Remote Trade

It is impossible for us to date too far back in history, because not only do we lack materials but there is also no need to do so. When it comes to peasants before the Ming Dynasty and the Qing Dynasty, they mainly used what they produced and were "forced to" exchange with others in a limited manner. As long as the peasants could produce something, they would not buy it. The simple appliances in a family, such as a stool, the wooden pig-pen, stove and so on, were made by the peasants. In addition, the cloth used to make clothes was weaved and spun by housewives. Before the Ming Dynasty (1368–1644) cloth was made from linen; after that, cloth was made from yarn. By the middle of the 19th century, about half of the rural households weaved their own cloth.[14] People even made white spirits which was regarded as luxurious. As the saying goes, "spirits are sold on the market, but the folks can make them at home",[15] "Every household has the tool to make spirits",[16] "Every household can make spirits".[17] They only come to the market to buy those which they cannot produce.

Local bazaars spread all over the country in rural areas, from ancient times till now. The bazaar was usually located at the center of several villages, the size of which varied according to the population and the local customs. Based on previous research, there was a bazaar in the center of every five to 10 villages in the southwest and there were even more bazaars in North China. One important standard is that the radius of the area covered is the distance traveled by walking back and forth in half a day (Li, 1957; Skinner, 1966). The bazaar was used to sell the handicraft of farmers, such as surplus cloth and things produced specially for family use like iron wares and paper.

[13]The handicraft industry in Jiangsu and Zhejiang was quite different from that in North China, which is more complicated. And I will discuss it in Chapter 4.
[14]The weaving households were the most around 1860, accounting for 45% of the total household (Xu, 1992).
[15]Bao, Shichen, *An Wu Si Zhong* (《安吴四种》) Volume 26; *Qi Min Si Shu* (《齐民四术》) Volume 2.
[16]Lu, Kun, *Qin Jiang Zhi Lue* (《秦疆治略》).
[17]Fang, Bao, *Qing Ding Jing Zhi Zha Zi* (《请定经制札子》), See *Fang Wangxi Quan Ji* (《方望溪全集》) "Other Articles" Volume 1.

Like other places in the world, these bazaars did not exist every day, usually twice in 10 days. In days without bazaars, if peasants needed to buy or exchange something with others, they resorted to the peddlers and craftsmen who moved from one village to another. They were an active part of the market and could deliver commodities and services to every corner of the village. What was common was a blacksmith shouldering a carrying pole with stove, peddlers shouldering groceries, masons, carpenters and even farriers.

Larger bazaars gathered around the county, where remote businessmen connected the local area with a larger region and even the whole country, because a county could not possibly produce all goods. Some products were limited by raw materials and locations, such as rush mats made of reed that could only be produced near the lake. Thus counties in the vicinity usually relied on the county providing rush mats. In this way, several, even dozens of counties relying on the county for rush mats formed a regional market. Wholesale businessmen were active in the market. In addition, big towns, suited at the center of water and land transportation, played a key role in the market.[18]

Trade at the national level at further distance than regional markets was very rare prior to the Ming and Qing Dynasties (1368–1912), which was mainly attributed to restrictions cast by place of origin for everyday needs, such as grain, salt and tea, etc. Sea salt was transported from the east to the southwest and northwest along the Yangtze River, while tea leaf was transported from the south to the north by sea transportation or by canal. However, due to the government's monopoly on the transportation of salt and tea over past dynasties, the long-distance trade at national level undertaken by businessmen were confined to the trade of some rare luxuries. Hence they were small in scale.

Prior to the Ming and Qing Dynasties, large bazaars like the fairs in medieval Western Europe were nowhere to be found in China. Although temple fairs in China could be considered a counterpart, they were held once or twice a year in one region. The development of the handicraft industry benefitted from the exchanges between different regions, especially the long-distance trades. In general, self-sufficient production in the handicraft

[18]Compared with the primary market, this fair contained distant commodities, which was the core of the market. It is called "Cao Shi" (rural fair) in the poem of the Song Dynasty (According to Wang, "a lot of commodities are presented in the fair, and taxes have to be paid by the maritime traders"). In the Ming and Qing Dynasties, the regional market was more and more active and frequent in the towns and counties than before.

industry promoted an active primary market (local market), and an active regional market with a larger scale or an active long-distance market was linked to the professionalism and expansion of the industry. The large-scale handicraft production and professional handicraft market had been absent in China for so long that Fernand Braudel doubts that they were needed at all as the local market could serve in their place (Braudel, 1985). If this state continued after the Ming and Qing Dynasties, one would stop expecting any signs of proto-industrialization. However, things changed fundamentally in the Ming Dynasty (1368–1644), with trade at the national level and in larger scale. One of the reasons was that cotton came to spread nationwide and its rapid circulation made its trade leap to a primary trade next only to grain. So this investigation starts from the Ming Dynasty and focuses on cotton cloth[19] which had the largest amount of trade.

South–North Mutual Transportation of Cotton in the Ming Dynasty (Before 1644)

Cotton and cotton textile industry were introduced to the Jiangnan Region in the Yuan Dynasty (1271–1368)[20] and popularized and extended in the Ming Dynasty. Instead of being extended nationwide, they were largely confined to the east with the southwest still focusing on hessian. The Yangtze River Delta (often called the Jiangnan Region) not only grew cotton widely but also enjoyed a high level of cotton textile industry. It transported large amounts of cotton to other regions, largely to regions like North China and the northwest where the weather is cold. Cotton was also grown widely in North China, but it failed to meet the regional needs. So cotton had to be bought from the Suzhou prefecture and Songjiang prefecture. Xu Guangqi (1562–1633) said, "Today, the cotton is cheap in the north while the cloth is expensive. The situation is opposite in the south. So cotton is shipped to the south while cloth to the north."[21] Thus one can see

[19]From the Ming and Qing Dynasties to the Republic of China, cotton took first place among the distant trade of domestic crafts. The distant trade of crafts except for cotton and silk were few in the Ming and Qing Dynasties, and more in the late Qing Dynasty, but cotton still took first place.

[20]The weaving technology was introduced by a woman called Huang Daopo from Hainan to her hometown Songjiang. In her lifetime, she made great efforts in advocating and improving the technology, and thus the Songjiang prefecture became the largest weaving area during the Ming and Qing Dynasties.

[21]Xu, Guangqi, *Nong Zheng Quan Shu* (《农政全书》), Volume 35.

that the southward transportation of cotton and northward transportation of cloth represent the large-scale circulation pattern of commodities. The cloth sold to North China and northwest is called "Biao Cloth" or standard cloth, which was durable, thick and warm. Thus it was the most prevailing cloth in the Jiangnan Region.

It has been said that the reason why cotton cloth was not self-sufficient in the cotton-producing North China is that it was technologically backward. As the saying goes "the north grows cotton well but does badly in spinning while the south does well in spinning but lacks cotton. So cotton is shipped to the south and cloth to the north".[22] But since the cotton spinning skills were easy to learn, the gap in technology was soon bridged in the Qing Dynasty. As cotton cloth became self-sufficient in North China, merchants dealing with standard cloth rarely came to Suzhou prefecture and Songjiang prefecture.[23] Since then, the mutual transportation of cloth and cotton between the south and north disappeared.

How many bolts of cotton cloth are transported to North China from Suzhou prefecture and Songjiang prefecture in the Ming Dynasty? To prove this, we can only use some fragmented materials. In *Yueshipian* (or "Seeing the World"), Ye Mengzhu records,

> "the bolt with broad and thin tip is standard cloth... All are transported along the roads leading to Shanxi province and the capital. Every bolt is about 1.5 *qian* (a *qian* equals to 5 grams) or 1.6 *qian* silver and the best one is about 1.7 *qian* or 1.8 *qian* silver at most... In the previous dynasty (Ming Dynasty), as the Biao cloth was prevailing, rich merchants came to buy them with large sums of money. They usually spent thousands of *liangs* (a *liang* equals to 50 grams) silver or hundreds of thousands of *liangs*. Even a sum hovering around ten thousand is small."

Merchants with hundreds of thousands of *liangs* were rare as most of them had tens of thousands of *liangs*. So Xu Dixin and Wu Chengming estimate that the total capital was 3 million *liangs*. If every bolt was about 1.5 or 1.6 *qian*, then the amount of cloth sold from Songjiang prefecture was no more than 20,000,000 bolts. With Jiading (in the north of Shanghai city) and Changshu (in the northeast part of Jiangsu province) which were abundant in standard cloth included, the total amount of cloth sold from the

[22]Wang, Xiangjin, *Mu Mian Pu* (《木棉谱》), documented in *Yuan Ming Shi Lei Chao* (《元明事类钞》), Volume 24.

[23]Ye, Mengzhu, *Yue Shi Bian* (《阅世编》). The merchant who sold the standard cloth (superior cloth) was called the standard merchant.

Suzhou prefecture and Songjiang prefecture were no more than 30,000,000 bolts (Xu and Wu, 1985).

However, not all cotton cloth was transported to the North, for part of them was transported to the northwest. Records often seen in the historical materials such as "Shanxi province and regions around the capital" and "Jiliao and Shanxi province"[24] usually refer to both North China and the northwest at the same time. Only the *Log of Changshu County* under the reign of the Emperor Jiajing of the Ming Dynasty (1507–1567) mentions that "... Six-tenths of the cotton cloth is bound and shipped to the regions once belonged to the state of Qi and Lu."[25] Here, the "regions once belonged to the state of Qi and Lu" refers to North China. Although the cloth produced in Changshu took up a small proportion of standard cloth produced in the Jiangnan Region, and the regions which once belonged to the state of Qi and Lu cannot represent the entire North China, six-tenths is a very rational ratio and the only clue. So I will do a calculation based on this ratio, then it can be seen that 18,000,000 bolts of the 30,000,000 bolts were sold to North China.

Cotton Cloth Trade in the Flourishing Times of the Qing Dynasty (1644–1840)

Before the First Opium War (1849), the Manchu people (the minority group dominating the Qing Dynasty) created flourishing times rarely seen in the history of China. These times are characterized by steadily growing population, increasingly flourishing domestic trade and per capita output of grain remaining at the highest level since the Song Dynasty (960–1279). In the Qing Dynasty, dramatic changes took place in the cotton textile industry. The cotton in North China was no longer transported to the south. Records in the Jiangnan Region say "no merchants come from the Jiangbei Region".[26] This is because the cotton textile industry in North China developed rapidly, achieved self-sufficiency, and was able to process local cotton. But this state was not accompanied by lack of cotton in the south, for the growing area in this region was expanded in the Qing Dynasty. According to literature, in the early and middle period of the Qing Dynasty, 70% to 80% of the farmland in regions like Songjiang prefecture,

[24] Wanli, *Log of Changshu County*, Volume 6.
[25] Jiajing, *Log of Changshu County*, Volume 4.
[26] Chuhua, *Mu Mian Pu* (《木棉谱》).

Taicangzhou, Haimengting in the Jiangbei Region and Tongzhou were used to grow cotton.[27]

Since cotton was no longer transported to the south and the cotton cloth in the Jiangbei Region was capable of self-sufficiency, the northward cotton transportation in the Jiangnan Region also rapidly shrank. "When it comes to our dynasty, merchants dealing with the standard cloth barely come. Recently, if any, they bring with them no more than tens of thousands of *liangs* of silver or gold, or two or three thousand *liangs* of silver or gold. And the profit is small."[28] It provides a stark contrast with what was mentioned in the Ming Dynasty. However, this did not lead to the decline of cotton textile industry in the Suzhou prefecture and Songjiang prefecture. Instead, they started to produce "thin cloth", which sold well in the Jiangxi, Hunan, Hubei, Guangdong and Guangxi provinces. It derived its name for it was thinner and cooler than the standard cloth. But the decline in selling and transporting of the standard cloth soon went by. After the reign of the Emperor Qianlong (1736–1796), the cotton from Jiangnan Region opened a new market in the northeast, embracing the comeback of the standard cloth on an even larger scale than the previous dynasty. Someone said that

> "all the seven cities benefit from the profit. ... The rich merchants from Hebei province bring with them large sums of money; with capital in hand, they rent or buy mules and horses travelling day and night in and out the region; when the rivers are frozen, they go to Suzhou and Changshu by boat along the Yangtze River. I learn that merchants from Suzhou selling cloth in the fall in the Song County, earning as much as 150,000 a day."[29]

What is described above is exactly the case of buying cloth from the south by carriages and boats. Based on this historical material, Xu Xinwu estimates in his *History of Homespun Cloth in the Jiangnan Region* that the Songjiang prefecture sold as many as 30,000,000 bolts of cloth annually in the flourishing times of the Qing Dynasty (Xu, 1992). Among the 30,000,000 bolts of cloth, half of them were the standard cloth sold to the north of Beijing and the northeast, while the rest were the "thin cloth" sold to Fujian province and Guandong province (Xu and Wu, 1985). This was just the case in Songjiang prefecture. If bolts of cloth produced in Changshu, Wuxi, and Jiading of Suzhou prefecture and Jiaxing of Zhejang province

---

[27] Gaojin, *Qing Hai Jiang He Mian Jian Zhong Shu* (《请海疆禾棉兼种疏》), *Huang Chao Jing Shi Wen Bian* (《皇朝经世文编》), Volume 37.

[28] Ye, Mengzhu, *Yue Shi Bian* (《阅世编》), Volume 7.

[29] Qinshan, *Song Wen* (《松问》), *Huang Chao Jing Shi Wen Bian* (《皇朝经世文编》), Volume 28.

are added, the annual number of bolts of cloth sold and transported by long distance in the Jiangnan Region will be about 40,000,000, an increase of 10,000,000 compared with that of the Ming Dynasty.

From the Ming to Qing Dynasty, North China achieved self-sufficiency by buying 18,000,000 bolts of cloth from the Suzhou prefecture and Songjiang prefecture annually. By the middle period of the Qing Dynasty, North China was one of the most common areas where peasants spun cloth on their own. Shi Jianyun looked up nearly 1,000 local historical logs of North China. From his quotation, we can see that the logs stretch 300 years from the reign of Emperor Jiaqing to the Republic of China (1912–1949) with self-spinning prevailing in the Kangqian flourishing times (the period when Emperor Kangxi and Emperor Qianlong were on the throne).[30] According to his calculation,

> "among the 329 county-level administrative units (including Sanzhou) in the Hebei, Shandong, and Henan province of the North China, 251 of them produce cotton and 227 of them produce cloth", and "the number of existing local logs in the North China is more than 1,600. I just look up less than 1,000 of them and there must be many historical materials concerning cotton textile industry not being included." (Shi, 1995: 335)

That is to say, in the Qing Dynasty, three-quarters of counties produced cotton (76%) and two-thirds produced cloth (69%), which was far beyond the average 45% nationwide.

Although spinning cloth by the peasants in North China was common, it is noticeable that the cotton textile industry in North China was quite different from that in the Jiangnan Region. In the Jiangnan Region, textile industry clustered in the counties and prefectures in the north of Taihu Lake, which was for the sake of sales. However, in North China, the cotton textile industry was evenly scattered among more than 200 counties in the Hebei, Shandong, and Henan province of North China, which was mainly for self-sufficiency. For peasants, spinning cloth meant making clothes to wear. They would sell the cloth in the local market for currency only if there was surplus. What is emphasized here is that for peasants, currency was needed merely to pay tax and family bills and no record shows that peasants tried to expand their production or buy farm lands from spinning cloth. In the

[30]See pp. 335–343 of *Handicraft Industry and Rural Economy* by Shi Jianyun. The cotton industry of Qing Dynasty is mainly described in this part, which is less stated in historical chronicles of Republic of China. So the description here does not include the Republic of China (Shi, 1995).

local logs, one often sees records about female peasants spinning day and night. For example, a poem goes

> "by the window, the loom continues to work to and fro, for tax comes one after another. It should be finished tonight even without sleep, for our village-chief will come tomorrow."[31]

In the poem, that the woman spins cloth at the expense of sleep was not because she wanted to sell it to cloth merchant, but because she had to change her cloth for currency in the local market to pay tax. Besides, currency was also extraordinarily important for peasants to attend to marriages and funerals. Men farmed to have enough food while women spun to cover daily expenditure. In addition, spinning could also help to provide food in places with a large population and insufficient food. Hence, the view goes "changing cloth for millet actually helps to provide food for poor people".[32]

To most of the peasants living in the North China Plain in the middle period of the Qing Dynasty, producing for self-use was the main purpose. In busy seasons, women might also do some farm work which was within their ability; and in winter when there was less farm work, men might also help with spinning. But one should not generalize spinning at the expense of sleep as a common scene for peasants. In the better part of a year, women were preoccupied with housework, and kept domesticated animals like chickens, ducks, pigs and sheep instead of merely spinning. In a situation where there was a lack of long-distance markets, surplus cloth would not be sold. Professional production was not possible unless the flourishing market was equipped with nationwide widespread business.

Fortunately, this kind of market focusing on long-distance sales could also be found in North China in the flourishing times of the Qing Dynasty. Our search of local logs shows that cotton textile industry in a few counties had attracted long-distance cloth merchants like that in the Jiangnan Region, and the main markets were in Shanxi Province and the northeast (Xu and Wu, 1985; Shi, 1995). Similar records are also found in about 13 to 14 counties, with a selling amount of 3 million bolts which was only one-tenth of that in Songjiang prefecture (Wu, 1985).

In the following section, I will shrink the investigating scope and take a close look at the situation in the dozens of counties involved in long-distance sales of cotton. By doing this, I aim to check whether they were similar to

[31]Guangxu, *Log of Wuqiao County*, Volume 11.
[32]Qianlong, *Log of Laoting County*, Volume 5.

the pro-industrialized regions in Europe or just at an even earlier stage than the pro-industrializing state. Proto-industrialization in the Jiangnan Region was relatively obvious and I will discuss it in the next chapter.

The Cotton of North China Was Exported to Distant Counties: The Beginning of Proto-industrialization

A lot of areas are considered as "proto-industrialization" areas by historians before the European Industrial Revolution. But there is still a lack of a common standard. According to Franklin F. Mendels, the most important feature of proto-industrialization was to produce for the distant market. However no one knows to what extent it will develop. By comparison, Hans Medick illustrates more on it. In an article related to proto-industrialization, he thinks the clearest standard is that the income of industry and sideline of most households exceed those of agriculture. In other words, the handicraft industry becomes the "owner" of the household, and all these are seen at the micro level. The macro-standard is that industry and sideline are considered as important parts of the total income, or the labor of industry and sideline are equivalent to those of agriculture.

Now let us analyze whether the weaving areas of North China met the standards mentioned above based on the local chronicles (quoted from Shi Jianyun).

There were two weaving areas in Zhili (the old name for Hebei Province in the Ming and Qing Dynasties), and the clearest was located in Luanzhou County and Laoting County of east Hebei. Most women of Luanzhou County were engaged in weaving as cotton was popular at that time, and the proportion of cotton for self-use was about two-tenths or three-tenths of the total, while seven-tenths or eight-tenths were for export sales. So cotton was an important source of the homespun income.[33] Laoting County was close to the frontier, so it focused mainly on export trade. Similarly, the production of cotton was export-oriented, with a proportion of eight-tenths or nine-tenths for export. In the slack season, men and women were engaged in weaving. Hence weaving gradually became the major source of work.[34] The largest cotton market was in the northeast which is north of the Shanhai Pass; the second-largest market was situated in the southwest

[33]Jiaqing, *Log of Luanzhou County*, Volume 1.

[34]According to the fifth volume of "Chronicles of Laoting County" in the Qianlong era, the weather in the north of China was dry which was difficult for weaving, so man tended to weave in the basement. But the statement is unbelievable.

of Hebei, including Luancheng County, Yuanshi County, Nangong County and Jingzhou County. The cotton was mainly transported to Shanxi and the northwest. Yuanshi County is close to Shaanxi, which was suitable for cotton. As a consequence, most men and women tended to be engaged in weaving, and the merchants were all there. Therefore, the cotton could be transported to the market as soon as the cloth was spun.[35] In Nangong County of the late Qing Dynasty, many merchants coming from Huguang areas (Hubei and Hunan Provinces) tended to weave with a lot of capital. During the reign of the Emperor Daoguang (1820–1850), most of women were engaged in weaving, and men tended to weave in the slack season. Although the production of cotton could not bring regular income, it was sufficient to support the whole family.[36]

The production areas mainly focused on Licheng which was near Jiana, Putai, Qidong and Guantao which were along the Yellow River. The cloth produced in Licheng County mainly included flat-bed machine cloth, wide cloth and small cloth. The flat-bed machine cloth was widely used, and the small cloth was shorter than the wide cloth, which was mostly sold at the frontier fairs. The wide cloth was more coarse and wider than flat-bed machine cloth which was suitable for making soldiers' clothes.[37] Besides agriculture, weaving was the most prosperous industry for the local people to live by. Hence many merchants from remote areas tended to make cotton exchanges there. During the period of Jiaqing (1796–1820), local people tended to do business at the fair, and hence the cloth market came into being. The amount of exchanged cloth a year in the northeast of China was about 100,000 bolts.[38] The cloth of Putai was divided into several types: half cloth, long cloth and cloth store. After achieving self-sufficiency, the local merchants started to open up a bigger market for the local people to live by.[39] In the middle of the Qing Dynasty which saw the prosperity of Guantao County, men tended to cultivate and women engaged in weaving, and the coarse cloth was popular and sold in Shanxi.[40] It is shown that the cotton of Shandong was mainly transported to the northeast of China, to Shanxi and Hubei.

[35]Qianlong, *Chronicles of Zhengding Prefecture*, Volume 12.
[36]Daoguang, *Chronicles of Nangong County*, Volume 10 & 6.
[37]Qianlong, *Chronicles of Licheng County*, Volume 5.
[38]Kangxi, *Chronicles of Qidong County*, Volume 8; Jiaqing, *Sequel Chronicles of Qidong County*.
[39]Qianlong, *Chronicles of Caozhou Prefecture*, Volume 7.
[40]The Republic of China, *Chronicles of Guantao County*, Part of Economy.

There are two areas producing cloth in Henan Province. One is Mengxian County and Mengjin County, north of the Yellow River. In the early Qing Dynasty, Mengxian County was famous for Meng cloth, and the merchants from Shaanxi, Gansu and north of the Yellow River came and bought the cloth.[41] Almost all the households of Mengjin County weaved the cloth, and the merchants of Shaanxi Province participated in it and put the product on the market.[42] The other weaving area was Zhengyang County, south of Henan, especially the Dou Goudian. Thus the cloth was called Dou cloth. Every household had a weaving machine; men and women were all engaged in weaving. Dou cloth was widely sold. To the east, it was sold to Henan Province; to the west, it was sold to Shanxi and Shaanxi.[43]

The distribution of weaving in three provinces of North China is seen in Table 3-3 (see page 53).

As is shown previously, these weaving areas are similar to the proto-industrialization area:

(1) The purpose of homespun production was for long-distance trade. The homespun produced in Shandong Province and the east Hebei Province were sold to the northeast of China, whereas the homespun produced in the southeast of Hebei and Henan Provinces were sold to Shanxi Province and then transported to the northeast. It went beyond the scope of local market and regional market, and started to produce for the distant market. Although the output of homespun of different counties was not clear, it is said that 70% to 80% homespun of Luanzhou and 80% to 90% of Laoting were for distant trade. There is no doubt that most of the homespun was for distant trade though no specific data of other counties are recorded.

(2) The textile industry was popular in the weaving area, and labor was no longer restricted to women. Among the 13 counties stated earlier, female labor was mentioned in four counties (Laoting, Yuanshi, Nangong and Zhengyang Counties). In addition, in Laoting County, the division of labor was such that women spun and men wove. The participation of male labor in weaving reflected the new job opportunities brought by the opening-up of the market, and it was a huge change.

(3) For some households, the cotton textile industry was turned from sideline to a major form of work, at least during the peak weaving

[41] Qianlong, *Chronicles of Mengxian County*, Volume 4.
[42] Jiaqing, *Chronicles of Mengjin County*, Volume 4.
[43] Jiaqing, *Chronicles of Zhengyang County*, Volume 9.

season. The woman weaving at home and the man weaving in the basement in Laoting County was recorded. Besides, the household depended much on weaving to make a living in Nangong County. So weaving was more important for the household than planting.

However, whether one can conclude that the phenomenon of proto-industrialization emerged in the North China Plain in the flourishing age of the Qing Dynasty is far from enough, according to Medick.

First of all, in terms of local macro-economy, the total output and sales were limited, and hence the total income cannot be compared with that of the planting industry. Although I do not have the homespun data of all the counties, the output was merely 100,000 bolts a year during the flourishing age of Qidong County, which is the base of North China. Wu Chengming estimates that the output was 3 million bolts. In the flourishing age of the Qing Dynasty, the scale was small, with less than 10,000 households. So even if every household had a weaving machine, the total output would only be 10 bolts of cloth.

Secondly, if it is estimated per year given that weaving had an obvious seasonal character, the participation of labor cannot be compared with that of agriculture. If it took six or seven days to weave a bolt of cloth, two or three months were needed for 10 bolts of cloth. As the homespun industry had an obvious seasonal character, only two or three months in a year were required to reach the high production mentioned earlier. My assumption can also be proved by the historical data mentioned. In Qidong County of Shandong Province, farmers tended to take the cloth to the fair and then sell it in May and June of the lunar calendar. In Zhengyang County of Henan Province, the night fair was set on a large scale, reflecting the prosperity of the local cloth fair. On the other hand, the booming phenomenon was not always seen all year round. The seasonal character of cloth production and sales reflects that agriculture played the most important role most of the time in a year. Among four counties of which man was engaged in weaving, two showed clearly that man tended to weave in the agriculture slack season. In other words, weaving was still a sideline even if it became the major work of households for two months. In addition, there was not a household which only lived or became rich by weaving. Instead, most households tended to cultivate and support themselves, and thus weaving cloth was not a specialized production.

On the whole, the weaving income and the participation of labor in the weaving areas of the north of China cannot be compared with those of European proto-industrialization, although we can still be aware of the appearance of proto-industrialization. Only after the development of foreign industrial products, domestic industrialization and urbanization in the late Qing Dynasty and early Republic of China, the weaving areas of North China had the characteristics of proto-industrialization so as to become a prosperous rural industrial area. However, the change took place in the industrialized era, so it is hard to consider it as proto-industrialization. Now let us discuss proto-industrialization of North China in the late Qing and early Republic of China, which was proto-industrialization appearing in the industrialized era.

Proto-industrialization in the Late Qing Dynasty and the Early Republic of China (1840–1937)

Wars frequently occurred in the hundred years after the First Opium War, and foreign industrial products were dumped into the domestic market. However, most of the domestic handicraft industries remained developing except for a small part.[44] In terms of the cotton textile industry, although several spinning industries completely declined, the manual weaving industry witnessed a great development. What is more, the pro-industrial weaving area was thus formed and can be compared with the rural industry area of Europe.

As is estimated earlier, in the flourishing age of the Qing Dynasty, the export sales of homespun a year for the north of China was 3 million bolts, 10 million bolts in Hebei Province in the late Qing Dynasty. In 1908, the sales of homespun was 4.44 million bolts, so Shi Jianyun considers the export sales of the north of China to be 20 to 30 million bolts, 10 times that in the flourishing age of the Qing Dynasty. Based on the result in *The Product Annals of Postal Area in the Republic of China*, in 1935, the export sales of Hebei was 9 million bolts, 12 million bolts in Shandong, and only a few hundred thousands in Henan,[45] with total sales of 24 million bolts,

[44]The hand-spinning, indigo-making, cloth-treading, traditional steel, original needle, candle, tobacco and board-printing industries were badly damaged (Xu and Wu, 1990: 902–908). Except for hand-spinning which was large-scaled, the rest were all small-scaled handicraft industry.

[45]The sales of homespun in Shandong Province was three times of those in the late Qing Dynasty because of the rise of the Weixian weaving area, with 10 million bolts of exported homespun yearly. This will be discussed in the following part. The reason for the low sales in Henan is unknown, or it may be due to wrong statistics.

Table 3-1 Export-oriented Trade of Cotton Cloth in Three Provinces of North China from the Ming Dynasty to the Republic of China (1368–1936)

	Ming Dynasty (million bolts) 1368–1644	Early and Middle Qing Dynasty (million bolts) 1645–1840	Late Qing Dynasty (million bolts) 1840–1910	The Republic of China (million bolts) 1911–1936
Zhili Province (Hebei Province)	—	—	10	9.80
Shandong Province	—	—	4.44	14
Henan Province	—	—	5	0.58
Total	18 (input)①	3②	20③	24

① according to Wu (1985).

② according to Wu (1985).

③ according to Shi (1995).

Sources: Wu (1985), Shi (1995), the General Post Office of Transportation Department (1937).

eight times as much as that in the flourishing age of the Qing Dynasty. The total output of homespun in the three provinces of the north of China from the Ming Dynasty to the early period of the Republic of China can be summarized in Table 3-1.

The results reflect the rapid development of production with the purpose of commodity output in North China. This phenomenon was quite different from the Ming and Qing Dynasties, because the homespun at that time still faced intense competition from foreign cloth and domestic machine-made cloth.

Foreign cloth was imported to China in the year of 1860, and the number doubled up by 1913. Later, it started to decline owing to the rise of domestic machine-made cloth. The domestic output was only 539.1 million in 1894, 409.67 million in 1936, 80 times of that in 1894 (see Table 3-2). Meanwhile, the total output of cotton started to decline in the 19th century because of foreign cloth, but it was not obvious in the 20th century when the machine-made cloth developed rapidly. According to Xu Xinwu, the output of homespun accounted for 65.17% of that of cotton in 1913, 71.45% in 1920, and 43.16% in 1936. In the 1920s and 1930s, the iron-wheel machine was popular in the rural homespun industry, but Xu Xinwu considers the cloth made by the iron-wheel machine as

Table 3-2 Development of Homespun Industry under the Competition from Both Machine-made Goods and Domestic Machine-made Cloth (1860–1936)

Item	Unit	1860	1894	1913	1920	1936
Import of machine-made cloth	Ten thousand bolts	1,988.4	9,169.6	25,361.2	20,399.3	10,777.1
Output of domestic machine-made cloth	Ten thousand bolts	—	539.1	1,756.0	3,663.6	40,967.0①
Homespun's percentage in expected output of cotton	%	96.82	85.85	65.17	71.45	71.00②

① The output of machine-made cloth includes many imitation ones, that is, homespun produced by the iron-wheel machine in 1936, thus the figure is much higher.

② Wu (1947).

Sources: Wu (1947); Xu (1992).

machine-made cloth[46] and underestimates the last two output numbers. According to other scholars, the proportion of homespun accounted for 61% to 78.5% of that of cotton,[47] and if one calculates based on 71%, the homespun industry was able to survive despite being faced with foreign cloth and machine-made cloth. As there are no other related estimates by scholars about the number in 1920, one shall rely on it for the moment.

Why was the homespun industry of North China able to keep its status faced with foreign yarn and machine-made cloth? Although a lot of explanations are given by scholars, the main one is that homespun competed with machine-made cloth in depending on cheap labor. The opportunity costs of weaving women were low, and they could not be employed by the labor market, so they had to be engaged in their own weaving (Zhao and Chen, 1977; Huang, 1990). To be specific, "if there was a weaving woman in a family, whether she wove or not, she must eat. What the meal cost was not included in the production cost, therefore, the family earned money."[48] In the 20th century, the development of homespun in North China depended

[46]The reason by Xu is insufficient. If the concept of the handicraft industry is only limited to the motive power acted on by manual labor, the iron-wheel machine belongs to the handicraft industry, because there was no manual driving device in it. Meanwhile, only Xu thinks that the iron-wheel machine does not belong to the handicraft industry.
[47]The proportion of homespun in the cotton is 43.2% (1936) by Xu, 78.5% (1930) by Fang, 71.1% (1933) by Wu, 61.0% (1935) by Yan (Xu, 1992; Fang, 1934; Wu, 1947; Yan, 1955).
[48]Shen, *Agricultural Book by Shen.*

mainly on the prosperity created by "proto-industrialization" instead of female labor regardless of cost.

The breakthrough took place at the end of the 19th century and the beginning of the 20th century. The situation about the three weaving areas of the north of China is all recorded in the literature of economic history. The centers of these three weaving areas respectively were Baodi County of Heibei Province, Gaoyang County and Weixian County of Shandong Province. They were all weaving areas rather than weaving counties, because these three counties were only the center of weaving areas, of which the influence also covered the surrounding counties. These three areas were very similar to European proto-industrialization in many aspects. Hence specific analyses should be made to discuss the output of homespun in weaving areas, the use of rural labor and the weaving income so as to demonstrate whether the breakthrough change and development were made compared with those of the weaving areas in the flourishing age of the Qing Dynasty.

Output of Commercial Cloth

Together with Xianghe County and Sanhe County, which are not far from Baodi County, Baodi County formed a Baodi cloth region, producing homespun cloth. At the end of the Qing Dynasty, a ballad went "Baodi is a big cloth-producing place; and Xianghe County is a small cloth-producing place". By adding the output of the three counties, one can get a total of about 2,000,000 bolts (Tianjin Archives, 1989: 971). During the early years of the Republic of China (1912), this cloth region embraced its heyday, with a sale of more than 4,800,000 bolts and markets covering 11 provinces (Shi, 1995: 354). Although cloth output in the region fluctuated with market, it still had a sale of 4,590,000 bolts by 1923. Due to the Japanese occupation of the northeast, the output started to decline rapidly, with 1,600,000 bolts by 1933 (Fang and Bi, 1936).

Gaoyang cloth region had a relatively large scope, reaching out to some villages in Renqiu County, Lixian County, Qingyuan County, Anxin County, Suning County and so on. It surged at a time later than that of Baodi. During 1916–1917, it embraced its heyday, with a sale of 4,000,000 bolts of homespun cloth.[49] It reached 5,500,000 bolts in 1928 and 3,000,000 bolts in 1929. Since then it remained around 1,000,000 to 2,000,000 bolts (Wu,

[49]The specification of homespun is different in Gaoyang and Baodi. Homespun in Baodi was narrow and small, and a laborer could weave 1.5 to 2 bolts every day, whereas homespun in Gaoyang was superior in weight and number. The scale and actual output of homespun in Gaoyang exceeded those in Baodi though the output was less than Gaoyang.

1936). By 1936, the total output of commercial cloth in Gaoyang reached 1,400,000 bolts.

The Weixian County cloth region also reached out to some villages in its surrounding counties, such as Changyi, Anqiu, Shouguang, etc. During 1915–1916, it had 500 traditional looms. By 1925, the number expanded to 50,000, with an annual output of 10,000,000 bolts, taking up one-third or a half of the total output in the entire North China (Ministry of Industry Bureau of Trade, 1933). Besides, no signs of decline were found after its homespun cloth rose rapidly. By 1936, a year before Japan invaded China; its annual output still reached 1,200,000 bolts.

From the aforementioned data, one can see the cloth sale in these regions all surpassed millions of bolts or tens of millions of bolts, enjoying a scale comparable to that in the Songjiang prefecture of the Ming and Qing Dynasties. From the macroscopic criterion of the proto-industrialization pointed out by Medick, one can see the handicraft industry output value of the three cloth regions took up about or more than 50% of the total industrial and agricultural output of the local place. In the early years of the 1930s, the handicraft industry output of Baodi, Gaoyang, and Weixian Counties took up 45.8%, 53.8%, and 48.4%, respectively[50] (Shi, 1995: 440–452).

Use of Labor Force

Let us have a look at the use of labor in the homespun cloth industry of these cloth regions. By doing this, one intends to check whether it was still characterized by strong seasonality like that in the flourishing times of the Qing Dynasty with the busy spinning season lasting only two months a year.

Similar to the flourishing times of the Qing Dynasty, peasants in these regions all had looms. So women were sure to engage in weaving. Then, what about men? Unlike the traditional textile industry, most of the instruments used in these emerging regions were iron-wheel machines.

[50]According to Shi Jianyun, the data of Hebei province were in 1931, the data of Shandong were in 1933, but we doubt the accuracy of the data. Taking Gaoyang as an example, in 1929, the total output of a cloth reached 30.6 million yuan (3 million bolts of clothes per year) (Fang and Bi, 1936). So in 1931, the output of homespun was 2 million, amounting to 20 million yuan (Wu, 1936), but based on the industrial statistics of Hebei in 1931 (the data used by Shi), the output value of the whole handicraft industry was only 6 million, while agricultural output value was 5.16 million. It is hard to identify which data are more accurate, but there is no doubt that the output value of the handicraft industry was higher than that of agriculture.

Instead of throwing shuttle by hand in the traditional way, the new looms were driven by pedaling the iron wheel. Male labor force was mainly used, for "great strength is needed and weak women are unable to do it" (Guang, 1935). Then how many male laborers were needed in these three regions?

To keep the iron-wheel machine functioning well, three people were needed, with a male spinning, and two women, a young and an old, slashing and combing warp and winding weft (Wu, 1936). In 1923, there were a total of 11,287 looms in the entire Baodi County. If each loom needed only one laborer, there would be about 11,287 men engaging in spinning. Due to lack of data concerning the total population and labor force then, one makes a rough calculation by using the statistical materials of 1930. The result is that the number of men engaging in spinning took up 50% of the total male population.[51] The ratio was larger in the Gaoyang region. From 1917 to 1927, the number of looms in Gaoyang increased from 13,000 to 27,000 and in the following few years (1927–1931), it remained above 20,000. If each loom needed only one laborer, it would be 75% or three-quarters of men in Gaoyang engaging in spinning. In the Weixian County, there were "more than 10,000 peasant households spinning, with about 40,000 looms and 80,000 to 90,000 men and women spinning and reeling respectively" (Peng, 1962b: 213). If each of the 40,000 men had a loom, the actual number of spinning men would be about 53%.[52] From this one can see there were at least half of the men engaged in spinning in this region. But the investigation should not be stopped here, for men engaging in spinning was seen even in the flourishing times of the Qing Dynasty. A more critical question is, how many days did these spinning laborers spend on spinning in a year?

In 1923, there were 11,287 looms and a total of 4,780,000 bolts of cloth. So one can deduce that every loom produced 424 bolts on average. Since the cloth produced in Baodi was narrow, it was smaller compared with the wide, improved cloth produced in the Gaoyang and Weixian Counties, and every loom could produce more than a bolt of homespun cloth a day. Therefore, if every loom produced 1.5 bolts a day, every peasant household with a loom would spend nine or 10 months on it. As for the wide, improved

---

[51] The total number of households is multiplied by the average population per household of Hebei, and then the total number of young laborers is that the former number is by the rate of 40%, and then the number of male young laborers is by 50%, so the number of young laborers was 22,600 for Baodi in 1930.

[52] Based on the statistics of government, it is estimated that the number of young laborers of Weixian County in 1930 was 150,000, among whom 70,000 were male laborers.

cloth in Gaoyang, producing one bolt a day would be very hard. One has not found any credible materials mentioning the spinning efficiency of peasant households in Gaoyang,[53] but one can figure it out by conjecture. In every bazaar,[54] its peasant households would deliver about three bolts to cloth merchants,[55] and a bazaar was held every five days. So they produced 0.6 bolts a day on average. Wu Zhi in his work guesses that each loom produced about 150 bolts every year. If the daily production was 0.6 bolts, 250 days would be needed. Thus, the spinning households in Gaoyang also spent eight or nine months a year mainly engaging in spinning. The situation in Weixian County was easier. In 1926, the entire county "produced about 40,000 bolts a day" and the annual output remained at 10 million bolts since then. So one can calculate that every loom needed to work for eight or 10 months in a row to complete it.

On the whole, in the three regions, not only half of their labor force was engaged in spinning but also spent eight to 10 months on spinning. Except time spent on sowing in the spring and harvesting in the autumn, they spent all the rest time on spinning. Compared with the flourishing times in the Qing Dynasty, the influence of seasonality had an obvious decline. Undeniably, spinning had taken up too much of the labor force and was mainly done by the male labor force. Then, how did the peasant households distribute their time in the agriculture and handicraft industries?

The answer to the question is similar to that of small private household business: hiring labor. According to existent materials of Gaoyang, the labor force market then was very prosperous and hiring labor was very common in spinning households. According to a local survey of Gaoyang in the 1930s, among the 382 spinning households, 154 of them hired labor or had apprentices, taking up 40.3% of the total; and the 154 households

[53]According to the statistics of homespun industry in Gaoyang, "In total, there are ten thousand cloth produced in Gaoyang. Most of the weaving machines are made in Gaoyang. If a laborer uses the machine to weave constantly, a bolt and 8 *cun* (1050 feet) of cloth can be made a day." In this way, in the flourishing age of Gaoyang, less than 30,000 bolts of cloth could be made, so the saying of 10,000 is unbelievable. The local iron-wheel machines were mainly from Tianjin, so it was not made locally. Wu Zhi thinks that three laborers are required to use a machine, but according to the description above, only one laborer is needed (Wu, 1936).

[54]"Fair" refers to the bazaar in rural areas. A large scale fair of Gaoyang County was on the fourth and ninth day of a month, whereas the common fair was every five days.

[55]Li mentions that every household sold two bolts of cloth in the fair before the year of 1910. During the Republic of China, with the popularity of the iron-wheel machine, the weaving speed started to increase, so three bolts of cloth were calculated according to Wu Zhi (Li, 1934; Wu, 1936).

had a total of 369 hired labor, with 24 laborers per household on average. Among all the spinning households, almost every household had one hired labor. Besides spinning, these hired labor would also help with farm work. Among all the hired labor, 192 specialized in spinning and 147 helped with farm work, taking up 40% of the total number. One can conjecture that spinning households could deal with both spinning and farm work well in busy seasons by hiring labor.

The flourishing textile industry and labor hiring made Gaoyang a rural industrial center, attracting peasants from neighboring regions and even other provinces to work there. According to the survey materials then, one finds that among the 369 hired labors, only 88 of them were locals, taking up less than a quarter; among the rest, 226 came from other counties and 55 from other provinces, taking up 61% and 15%, respectively.

From this material, we can see that the textile industry made Gaoyang a small rural industrial district. Not only did the local peasant households spend a lot of labor and time on it but also many laborers from neighboring areas were attracted to work there. It was a perfect example of Smithian Growth and rural industrialization.

Income from Spinning

Let us look at Baodi first. In 1923, the ratio of income from spinning and agriculture was 80:20 to a sharecropper engaging in spinning, which means "the former is about 3 times more than the latter"; and for a yeoman, the income from spinning was also higher than that from farming, with a ratio of 1:0.7, so it is obvious that income from spinning was higher than that from farming (Fang and Bi, 1936).

When the iron-wheel machine first emerged in the early years of the Republic of China, peasants spinning and selling on their own used foreign yarn to spin wide cloth and could earn 200 *diaos* (a monetary unit in the Ming and Qing Dynasties) while the annual income of a farming hired labor then was merely 20 *diaos*. If one includes the board expenses (the practice in Gaoyang was that long-term hired hands could live and eat in the peasant's home),[56] their total income would be about 40 *diaos*; and if 2.5 persons worked on each loom, each could get 80 *diaos*, still twice of the income

[56] See the Agriculture part of *Statistical Abstract of the Republic of China* (《中华民国统计提要：廿四辑》) (DGBAS national government, 1936) (国民政府主计处).

of long-term hired hands (Wu, 1936). By the early years of the 1930s, the peasant household in Gaoyang earned about 0.775 a day according to the survey conducted by the School of Economics of Nankai University (Wang, 1935). If 2.5 laborers worked on each loom for 300 days, the annual net income of each labor would be about 90–100 yuan. In 1933, the average income for long-term hired labor in Hebei Province was about 30 yuan. Apart from board expenses, income from spinning was still obviously higher than income from farming labor.

Compared with the above, Weixian County had the fewest materials, so one only deduces that by spinning a bolt of cloth, a peasant would earn a silver dollar (Peng, 1962c: 212). One has already seen that every loom in Weixian County produced about 250 bolts of cloth. If 2.5 laborers worked on each loom, every laborer would have a net income of 100 silver dollars a year. One cannot find out the annual net income of farming labor in the county, but in 1933, every male farming labor earned about 40 silver dollars in Shandong Province. So it is undoubted that income from spinning was higher than that from farming.

The above is a comparison between a laborer's net income from spinning and his net income from farming. In the annual net income of a household, spinning had become the principal work. Wu Zhi did a survey targeting 344 spinning peasant households in 1936. In every household, the net income from spinning was 120.71 yuan, and that from farming was 27.96 yuan and the income from other sideline production was 4.24 yuan. The income from spinning took up 78.94% of the total net income of a peasant household, from which one can see its importance (Wu, 1936).

One can summarize and list the above output of homespun cloth, use of labor and income in Table 3-3. From the table, one can clearly see obvious change had taken place in the spinning activity of the three cloth regions compared with traditional society.

Firstly, the labor force started to shift from agriculture to handicraft industry and agriculture in these cloth regions was degraded to a secondary position. Similar to the effects brought about by rural industrialization in the early days of the 1980s, the income per land began to increase with land and population pressure lessening, which is reflected in the income of farming hired labor in these cloth regions being obviously higher than that of other provinces or the average income of the province.

Secondly, handicraft industry started to get rid of involution. In the three cloth regions, the net income from spinning was about two to three times more than that from agriculture (both with board expenses

Table 3-3 Information on the Three Big Weaving Areas in North China①

	Baodi Weaving Area	Gaoyang Weaving Area	Weixian Weaving Area	Average
The number of counties covered	3	10	3	5.3
Output of commercial homespun				
1911	480	Not clear	Few	—
1916–1917	Not clear	400	Not clear	—
1923–1928	400–500	500	More than 1,000	More than 650
1933–1936	100–200	100–200	More than 1,000	More than 430
The percentage of handicraft industry gross value in industrial and agricultural total output (%)	45.8	53.8	48.4	49.3
The percentage of weaving male in the total amount of male labor (%)②	50.0	75.0	53.0	59.3
The time spent on weaving in a year (months)	9–10	8–9	8–10	9
The percentage of weaving income in total income (%)	58.8	78.9	Not clear	—
The weaving wages of every labor/agriculture's average wages in the province ratio③	57:30④	95:30	100:40	—

① Except special circumstances, the statistics here are from the 1930s. Statistics on the use and income of labor tells us about the situation in the central counties of the three weaving areas, that is, Baodi County, Gaoyang County, and Weixian County. One could not calculate the usage and income of labor in other counties because of lack of relevant materials.

② The statistics in Baodi is the total income, while that of Gaoyang is net income.

③ Suppose the annual pay of agricultural Changgong in the 1930s was 30 yuan and that of Shandong was 40 yuan, not inclusive of food expenses. If food is included, the annual pay of agricultural Changgong was about 50 yuan and that of Shandong 70 yuan.

④ Statistics here is from 1923.

Sources: Directorate-General of Budget, Accounting and Statistics (1936); Wu (1936); Fang and Bi (1936); Peng (1962b, 1962c).

subtracted). In the cloth-spinning region, the income from spinning of a female laborer was obviously higher than the income of a male farming laborer in other regions of the province.[57] Thus it will be justifiably called "industrialization".

From a detailed investigation made in the three cloth-spinning regions, the handicraft industry in these regions were similar to the pro-industrial region in Europe, perhaps even at a higher level. In these industrial regions, one cannot find "involution" any more, for both the spinning households and the hired labor from far away all produced for the largest profit. As for the reason concerning the forming and emerging of these industrial regions, I will discuss them in Chapter 5. In the next chapter, I will turn to the south to study proto-industrialization in the Jiangnan Region.

[57]Gender differences are not taken into consideration in calculating the income of every laborer, while it is estimated by 2.5 laborers per machine, so the income is the same for both men and women.

Chapter 4

"Involution" and "Industrialization": Investigation of the Cotton Textile Industry in the South of the Yangtze River

In the previous chapter, the industrialization process of rural areas in the north of China was investigated, and it was found that some rural areas there began a process similar to proto-industrialization in Western Europe until the early 20th century, when the manufacturing industry spread on a large scale. Now let us move the attention to the rural industry of the Yangtze River Delta. The question to be answered here is very similar to that in the previous chapter: was the rural industry the start point or result of agricultural involution there if it did exist? To what extent can the rural industrialization be called proto-industialization?

To answer this question, the key is the degree of labor transfer to the cotton textile industry and the net profit of laborers carrying on cotton textile work, which was quite similar to the work done in the previous chapter. If the return to laborers of the cotton textile industry was higher than the average income of the labor market, and the mass of laborers entering the cotton textile industry was on a large scale, the cotton textile industry should be defined as flourishing industrialization rather than the sideline of peasant households or an involutionary industry with a diminishing profit. Let us start from the late Ming Dynasty to reveal the change in different historical stages in the cotton textile industries of Songjiang prefecture and the surrounding areas.

The "Female Industrialization" of Songjiang Prefecture in Ming and Qing Dynasties (1573–1840)

Population and Land

It is hard to ascertain the situation of the early and middle Ming Dynasty, and thus the investigation in this chapter covers about 250 years of history, from 1573–1839, the eve of the First Opium War. This period is the most prosperous of the Western original industrialization (Mendels, 1972; Kriedte *et al.*, 1981). Based on the historical developments and statistics of Songjiang prefecture, the period can be divided into three stages, namely, the late Ming and early Qing Dynasty (from 1583 to 1663), the flourishing age of the Qing Dynasty (from 1662 to 1795) and the boom-bust stage of the Qing Dynasty (from 1796 to 1939).

This chapter deals with the cotton textile industry, especially in Songjiang prefecture. Songjiang prefecture is situated on the estuary of the Yangtze River of China, equivalent to today's Shanghai and its surrounding rural areas. In the Ming Dynasty, Songjiang prefecture included Huating and Shanghai County. Then Qingpu County was added in the early Qing Dynasty, and then these counties were divided and merged, totaling eight counties till 1816. Although it had witnessed an increase in the number of counties, these counties were all divided from one county; little change can be seen in other regions and population because of administrative division. The situation of population and land of Songjiang prefecture in the aforementioned three periods are shown in Table 4-1.

As is shown in the table, from the late Ming Dynasty prior to the Opium War, the population of Songjiang prefecture grew quickly,[58] whereas there was little change and even decrease in land. Meanwhile, the land of each household and per labor was also reduced. The land in the Qing Dynasty only amounted to half of that in the Ming Dynasty, and less of that in the Emperor Jiaqing's era. Based on the standard of "one farmer can only cultivate ten acres of land"[59] made by Zhang Luxiang during the late Ming and early Qing periods, an ordinary farmer could cultivate eight acres of land, which was an appropriate proportion of labor and land in Songjiang

[58]The previous census of Jiaqing mainly includes male population and female population related to land tax instead of the total number of population. According to the survey, the population in the late Ming Dynasty is not the real number, so it is more exact if we calculate the average land of labor on the basis of the number of households instead of male and female numbers (Cheng, 1989).

[59]Zhang Lvxiang, *Bu Nong Shu* (《补农书》).

Table 4-1 Population and Land of Songjiang Prefecture during the Three Periods

Periods Time Span	From the Late Ming Dynasty to the Early Qing Dynasty 1573–1661	The Heyday of the Qing Dynasty 1662–1795	From Emperor Jiaqing to Emperor Daoguang in Qing Dynasty 1796–1839
Number of households	21,859	299,659①	380,959②
Population	484,414	—	2,038,133③
Land	4,247,703	4,148,278④	4,048,871
Average land of every household	19.45	13.84	10.63
Average land of every labor (male labor)	12.35⑤	8.63	6.62

① There is no statistics about the number of households of Songjiang prefecture in the Qing Dynasty and the figure here is an estimate from the average between statistics at the end of the Ming Dynasty and the early Qing Dynasty and years from Emperor Jiaqing to Emperor Daoguang.

② The number of households in Emperor Jiaqing's era is calculated by the total population. The average number of people in a household — 5.35 persons — is calculated by the average between "average 5.25 persons in a household" in Songjiang prefecture at the end of the Ming Dynasty and "average 5.45 persons in a household" in the early Republic of China.

③ The population from Emperor Jiaqing's era to Emperor Daoguang's era is calculated by the average of only two figures, that is, the population in the 15th year and that of the 21st year in Emperor Jiaqing's era.

④ There is no statistics about the area of land of Songjiang prefecture in the zenith of the Qing dynasty. Here the figure is an estimate of the average figure at the end of the Ming dynasty and in Emperor Jiaqing's era.

⑤ In history, there is no statistics about the number of male labor in a household. Here it is estimated that 30% of the number of people in a household are male labor.

Sources: All the information above comes from Liang (1980) except estimated statistics.

prefecture in the flourishing age of the Qing Dynasty, and the phenomenon of relative labor surplus occurred during the period of Emperors Jiaqing and Daoguang.

Prosperous Cotton Textile Industry

It is supposed that the cotton cloth of Songjiang prefecture was first produced in the late Ming Dynasty. As estimated by Wu Chengming, the foreign sales of cotton cloth was about 20 million in the late Ming Dynasty (Wu, 1985). So how many people were needed?

In the sixth year of Wanli of Ming Dynasty (1578, 66 years before the downfall of the Ming Dynasty), there were 218,359 households in Songjiang prefecture, more than 200,000 of households in the late Ming Dynasty. As calculated in the Wanli era (1573–1620), 92 bolts of cotton cloth were produced in each household of Songjiang prefecture in the late Ming Dynasty.[60] If there were two women in each household[61] (mother and daughter-in-law were common), one bolt cloth can be made in three and a half working days,[62] and thus it took several months, almost 322 days to make 92 bolts of cloth. In the early Qing Dynasty, the cloth of Songjiang prefecture was mainly exported to central China and south China instead of the northern part of China. During the period of Qianlong (1735–1795), sales in the north of China turned out to be flourishing because of the opening-up of the northeast market, with at least 20 million bolts of cloth. In the Jiaqing era (in the early 19th century), there was a great growth in the sales of cotton cloth in Songjiang prefecture, reaching 30 million[63]; besides, there were 10 million bolts of cloth in the Changshu prefecture, 3 million in Wuxi county, 40 million in the south of the Yangtze River (Wu, 1985). In the 15th year of Emperor Jiaqing (1810), the population of Songjiang prefecture was up to 1,591,539, and the output of cloth was 19 bolts per person in a year. If there were 5.35 laborers in each household,[64] and it was necessary for each household to make 102 bolts of cloth a year — 10 bolts of cloth more than that in the late Ming Dynasty, as calculated by two women in each household — it took only six days to make a bolt of cloth in the Qing Dynasty, for a total of 306 days, namely more than 10 months.

[60]There were only 2.2 people in a household, far less than those in China which had five people in a household, so we calculated it by household instead of number of people.
[61]Based on the data, female labor amounts for most labor in the cotton textile industry in Songjiang areas, whereas male labor was rare. I will analyze it in the following parts.
[62]It takes a laborer four days to spin, one day to slash, one day to weave, totaling six days (Yan and Wu, 1985). These are the statistics of the Qing Dynasty. According to Li Bozhong, the efficiency was lower in the Ming Dynasty, so it took seven days to weave a bolt of cloth (Li, 1997).
[63]These are the statistics of 1805 (Xu, 1992), so the average output is calculated by the population in 1810 instead of 1816.
[64]The statistics of household was not unified during the whole period of the Qing Dynasty. Only the household number at the beginning (1626) and the end (the beginning of the Republic of China, 1911) of the period is clear, respectively 5.25 and 5.45. It is estimated that there are five people in a household, so we choose the average of these two numbers, 5.35 (Liang, 1980).

It seems that during the 200 years from the late Ming Dynasty to the middle of the Qing Dynasty (about 1578–1810), the cotton textile industry in the south of the Yangtze River, especially Songjiang prefecture kept on developing. There were at least two people in each family engaging in weaving all year round, which is similar to the wool textile industry in some rural areas of Western Europe during the same period. What about the income of the textile industry? Was it a commodity production of high income, or daily subsidiary business for the farmer to make a living?

The income of the textile industry can be investigated in the following two aspects. First, whether the absolute level of income allowed laborers to simply maintain a living. One of the economic characteristics of involution is that the output is only enough to make ends meet, which was the inevitable result of population pressure and surplus labor force. In addition, comparison should be made of the marginal output of the cotton textile industry and agricultural labor. If the former was higher than the latter, it is shown that industrialization came into being. In this way, the cotton textile industry gradually absorbed the surplus labor from agriculture.

Marginal Income

There is little discussion about the income of the cotton textile industry before the First Opium War, such as "it was enough to maintain the life of two people", "it was enough to support a whole family of eight", "the income of cotton textile industry was higher than that in agriculture". In terms of influence, it is believed that the income of cotton cloth was similar or higher than agricultural income. However, it is hard to define without quantity support. If one is to estimate the net income of each cloth in detail, one has to estimate on the basis of previous quantity surveys. As of now, there are two scholars making detailed estimates on the income of the cotton textile industry in the south of the Yangtze River in the Ming and Qing Dynasties. The results are in the fourth and fifth columns of Table 4-2.

The results show that the estimates of these two scholars on the income of the cotton textile industry in the south of the Yangtze River in the Ming and Qing Dynasties are different. In my opinion, deviation exists in the estimates of both scholars. The scholar surnamed Wang underestimates the income with inappropriate method, whereas the other scholar surnamed Li

Table 4-2 Net Income of Every Bolt of Cloth in the Cotton Textile Industry in the South of the Yangtze River during the Ming and Qing Dynasties (Bushel of Rice)

Period	Chinese Era Name	Time Span	Estimated by Mr. Wang	Estimated by Mr. Li	My Revision
From the late Ming to the early Qing Dynasty	Wanli	1573–1620	1.4	—	1.4
	Early years of Tianqi	1621	1	—	1.4
The heyday of the Qing Dynasty	Early years of Kangxi	1662–1690	0.9	2.3	1.45
	Late Kangxi period	1690–1722	—	1.4	—
	Early and middle period of Qianlong	1736–1776	1.05	1.9	1.6
Turn of heyday to recession	From Jiaqing to Daoguang	1796–1839	0.6	1	1

Sources: Wang (1993); Li (1997).

overestimates the income, and both should make corrections.[65] The result of correction is set in the sixth column. It is shown that in the periods of the late Ming Dynasty and the early Qing Dynasty, and the flourishing age of Qing, the net income of a bolt of cloth amounted to 1.5 bushels of rice after deducting raw material prices, which remained stable for 200 years.

[65]Although Wang Tingyuan defines the specification of standard cloth in detail at the beginning of his article, there are still some problems about the definition. According to Ye Mengzhu of the Qing Dynasty, the width of cloth is 1.2 *chi* (1 *chi* = 1,0936 feet), which is similar to Xu Xinwu, the length is about 20 *chi*, weighing 16 to 20 *liang* (16 *liang* = 1 *jin*), with 1 *jin* of oil consumption (Ye, 1981; Xu, 1992). However, Wang Tingyuan thinks that the standard cloth weighed above two *jin*, because the cloth sold in the north was larger than that in the south, and the price of standard cloth was much higher than that of the small cloth. She does not mention that the high price of standard cloth was for the thick texture instead of large scale which was more suitable for the weather in the northern part of China. On the contrary, the texture of small cloth in the south was sparse, so the price was half of that of the standard cloth. There is something wrong with the definition of Wang Tingyuan, so the net income he estimates is lower than actual income. Li does not calculate it, but adopts the results of Fang (1987), Zhongshan and Wang (1993). The specification of homespun, the price of rice, cotton and cloth are different, so the estimates of Li in the table are different in different ages. Based on the price of rice, cotton and cloth of Wang, I will try to calculate the net income of a cloth with the cost of 1 *jin* of cotton instead of 2 *jin* of cotton.

However, in the period of Jiaqing, the net income reduced by 50%. My estimate is similar to that of historical text data.

In the Qingpu County of Songjiang in 1667, "farmers in Qingpu County weaved a bolt of cloth, by 3 jin (1 jin = 0.5kg) of cotton. Therefore, if we use 4 jin of cotton, the cost of 3 jin of it is the price of the cloth and the rest is labor fee."[66] That is to say, the net income is three-fourths of the cloth price. During the early years of the Kangxi era (1661–1722), the cloth price is 2 *qian* (1 *qian* = 0.1 *liang*), and the price of cotton was 0.55 copper per jin. One jin of cotton could be used to weave a bolt of cloth. So the net income was 1.45 *qian* after deducting the cotton cost. At that time, the price of a bushel of rice was 1 *qian*, so the net income of cloth-weaving was 1.4 bushels of rice, three times the price of cotton.

During the period of Xianfeng (1850–1861), it is said that 3 jin of cotton were made into one bolt of cloth, so a bushel of rice should be used to exchange 3 jin of cotton. It proves that, during this period, the net income of a bolt of cloth was always a bushel of rice, three times as much as that of raw material because the price of cotton reduced. Since the price of rice began to rise, a bolt of cloth could not be exchanged for a bushel of rice.

The net income of a cloth is clear, so one can calculate the marginal net output of a weaving labor. If there were two female laborers in each household in the Ming and Qing Dynasties, it might take them 10 months a year to reach the average level of production (92 bolts of cloth at the end of the Ming Dynasty, 102 in the Jiaqing era). If there were less than two female laborers in each household, it was still hard to make 100 bolts of cloth despite working all year round. So if every woman could work 300 days a year, the income of weaving amounted to 2.5 litres of rice before the Jiaqing era (about 1800), 1.7 litres of rice after the Jiaqing era, which was the marginal output of a female laborer.

Was the marginal net output of the textile industry higher than the marginal output of agriculture? Let us calculate the marginal output of agricultural work of a yeoman, sharecropper and farm laborer (or *changgong*, also known as "long-term laborer"), respectively.

The Marginal Output of Agricultural Work

In the late Ming Dynasty, each household of the Songjiang prefecture had 19.45 acres of land to cultivate, up to 10.63 acres of land till the Jiaqing era of the Qing Dynasty. If it is calculated by "a household cultivates

[66] Lu, Shiyi, *Fu Ting Xian Sheng Wen Chao* (《桴亭先生文钞》), Volume 5.

10 acres of land" (Liang, 1980; Li, 1993; Li, 1997), the output of paddy is 2.5 *dan*[67] (1 *dan* amounts to 10 bushels, 1 bushel amounts to 10 litres); in the floурshing age of the Qing Dynasty, the output of paddy should be 3 *dan*[68]; the output of polished rice should be 1.75 *dan* in the late Ming Dynasty, and 2.1 *dan* in the Qing Dynasty. At the end of Ming and the early Qing, bi-annual planting of wheat and paddy was popular. The output of wheat was 1 to 1.5 *dan* per acre, but not very stable. According to Zhang, it was uncommon to see that the output of rice was 3 *dan* per acre, and wheat was 1.5 *dan* per acre. In general, 3 *dan* was normal.[69] According to Li Bochong (1997), the output in the Qing Dynasty was overestimated as 3.7 *dan*, since the output of wheat was calculated as 1 *dan* of wheat, which amounted to 0.7 *dan* of rice, adding 3 *dan* of paddy. However, the latter was not converted into polished rice. The output of wheat was not that stable, and hence it can be calculated as 0.5 *dan*, which amounted to 0.35 dan of rice. Hence, the output per acre was about 2.5 *dan* in Songjiang in the Qing Dynasty combined with 2.1 *dan* of polished rice.

If a man cultivated 15 acres of land[70] of a household in the late Ming Dynasty,[71] he could get 26.25 *dan* of polished rice, which came down to 15.75 *dan* after deducting the production cost (mainly seed, fertilizer),[72] and amounted to 4.3 litres of rice per day. In the Qing Dynasty, "one farmer only can cultivate ten acres of land",[73] if it was calculated by 10 acres, 2.5 *dan* were produced per acre, totaling 25 *dan*, which came down to 18 *dan* after deducting the cost, and amounted to 5 litres of rice. Therefore,

---

[67]He, Liangjun, *Si You Zhai Cong Shuo* (《四友斋丛说》), Volume 14.

[68]Jiang, Gao, *Pu Liu Zi Nong* (《浦柳咨农》), "In general, the output per mu is about 3 *dans*."

[69]Zhang, Lvxiang, *Nong Shu* (《农书》).

[70]Although the cultivated land per household of Songjiang prefecture in the late Ming Dynasty was as much as 19 mu of land, it was about 15 mu in the whole south of the Yangtze River. Scholars always calculate it by 15 mu of land, so I will try to calculate by 15 mu.

[71]According to *Chronicles of Jindi*, in the late Ming Dynasty, a couple of Jiangxi County cultivated 25 mu of land, of which man could cultivate 15 mu based on the different ability of man and woman. The spring system was not widespread in the Ming Dynasty, so it was feasible that a man could cultivate 15 mu of land. Meanwhile, the cultivated land per household was 14.5 in the late Ming Dynasty, as is calculated by one man per household; 15 mu of land could be cultivated.

[72]According to Li (1997), the production cost was beyond 1 *dan*, which amounts to 0.7 *dan* of rice, so the cost of 15 mu of land and 10 mu of land were respectively 10.5 and 7 *dan*.

[73]According to Zhang (1983), bi-annual planting was popular in the late Qing Dynasty, with high demand of labor.

4.3 litres and 5 litres were the marginal output of yeomen in the late Ming Dynasty and Qing Dynasty, which were much higher than that of weaving.

One tends to investigate whether the income of the farmers south of the Yangtze River in the Ming and Qing Dynasties was only enough for them to make a living. In general, a household with five people and 10 acres of land could only rely on male labor to gain 5 litres of polished rice per day, which was sufficient for a household. If there were still other one or two women engaging in the cotton textile industry, the annual income amounted to 750 litres — 1500 litres of polished rice in the late Ming Dynasty and the flourishing age of the Qing Dynasty, 510 litres — 1020 litres of polished rice in the Jiaqing era. It shows that the development of the cotton textile industry was the key factor to the high living standard of Songjiang. Meanwhile, it also proves that the input of farmers in the cotton textile industry was to produce commodity for the market instead of maintaining their living standard.

This was about the situation of yeomen. If one wants to make clear the opportunity cost of weaving, there is a need to compare the marginal output of weaving with that of yeoman and laborer, because the price of the latter can reflect the true price of labor in an area, which makes it possible for us to make out whether the agricultural work of the area would be transformed to handicraft industry.

Suppose a farmer of the Qing Dynasty rent 10 acres of land, he would gain 18 *dan* of polished rice deducting the cost of production. The rental was 1 *dan*,[74] which amounted to 0.7 *dan* of polished rice, so 11 *dan* was left after deducting the rental; the net income was equal to 3 litres of rice. If the farmer hired a laborer, the wage and meal expenses were 11 *dan* of rice equivalent to 3 litres in the late Ming Dynasty,[75] and about 13 *dan* of rice equivalent to 3.6 litres in the middle of the Qing Dynasty. A long-term laborer was more laborious than a sharecropper, and hence the wage of the former was inevitably higher than the latter.

The main laborers of agriculture were men, whereas the primary laborers of textile were women. Therefore, the influence of gender difference should not be ignored to compare the net income and opportunity cost of these two industries. The differences are demonstrated in the following two aspects.

[74]In the flourishing age of the Qing Dynasty, Li (1993) thinks that the rice which was paid as land taxes was 1 *dan* per acre. Wang holds the same view (1993).
[75]Zhang, Lvxiang, *Bu Nong Shu* (《补农书》).

Table 4-3 Comparison of Marginal Net Income (the Amount Consumed Deducted) (Litre of Rice)

Periods Time Span	From the Late Ming Dynasty to the Early Qing Dynasty 1573–1661	The Heyday of the Qing Dynasty 1662–1795	From Emperor Jiaqing to Emperor Daoguang in Qing Dynasty 1796–1839
Weaving women	1.15①	1.5	0.7
Sharecropper	—	1.67	—
Changgong (farm laborer hired by the year)	1.4	1.94	—
Yeoman	3	3.6	—

① We estimate that every woman weaved 46 bolts of cloth, and the net value of each bolt of cloth was 1.4 bushels of rice. After deducting 3 *dan* of rice (180kg) as food, the net income of weaving cloth was 3.44 *dan* of rice (206.4 kg), 1.15 litres of rice every day.

First, man and woman differ in food intake, so the food intake of woman should be deducted in the process of calculating marginal net income of textile industry. Relatively, the food intake of man should also be deducted in agricultural activities, which is helpful to the comparison of net income. Based on the different food intake of man and woman, the marginal net income is modified in Table 4-3.

It is suggested in the table that the food intake of a woman was about 1 litre of rice per day,[76] man about 6 *dan* of rice,[77] namely 1.6 litres per day. Meanwhile, that of a male sharecropper and yeoman were 5 *dan* of rice, which amounted to 1.4 litres per day.

As the table suggests, in the flourishing age of the Qing Dynasty, the marginal net income of a male sharecropper was 20% higher than that of a female laborer. Why did woman not participate in agricultural work?

A second aspect of gender difference should be taken into account. The different productivity of man and woman in cultivation and weaving led to

[76] Based on Volume 26 of *Four Aspects of Anwu* written by Bao, in Suzhou prefecture of Jiaqing era, everyone had to eat 3 *dan* of rice. Li thinks that a person at that time may consume 3.6 *dan* of rice each year, which amounts to a litre of rice a day (Li, 1997).

[77] As is described in *Book of Shen*, a long-time laborer in Jiaxing area may consume 5 *dan* and 5 bushels, firewood and wine of one *liang* and two *qian*. The firewood can be counted into production cost, and wine is counted into meal expenses, totaling six silvers which amount to 6 bushels of rice, so the meal expenses of a long-time laborer were 6 *dan* and one bushel (Zhang, 1983). If the cultivation was for their own household, the cost of wine and rice was saved, so the meal expenses of sharecropper yeomen were 5 *dan*.

high opportunity cost of man's changing from cultivation to weaving, and woman's turning from weaving to cultivation. Let us see the opportunity cost of a woman in weaving first.

If a woman were to engage in agricultural production, the marginal output was just half of a man.[78] Based on the previous calculation method, at the end of the Ming and the early Qing Dynasty, the marginal net income should be 0.52 litres of rice after deducting the cost of meals, 0.8 litres of rice in the flourishing age of the Qing Dynasty, which only amounted to 45% to 55% of that in the textile industry. That is to say, if a woman gave up weaving and turned to cultivation, she could only get half of the net income.

Let us discuss the opportunity cost of a male laborer engaging in agriculture. First, in the Ming and Qing Dynasties, the man–land ratio of the south was higher than that of other areas. But the output per unit area was higher because of intensive cultivation. As shown in Table 4-3, a male yeoman could plant 10 acres of land. Some of the net income can be used to support himself, and the rest was about 33.6 litres of rice, which can support the other three people. Before the Jiaqing era, each male laborer could cultivate 8.63 acres of land, and so the situation of male labor surplus was not serious. Meanwhile, the nature of the textile industry was different from that of agriculture. In the textile industry, the main work — spinning was suitable for women, which required coordinated movement and average force. If men were to engage in spinning, the marginal output would not be improved. But in terms of weaving, men were more competent for their high efficiency. On the other hand in the Ming and Qing Dynasties, farmers tended to use old picking machines, and thus they had to pick with their hands, which was different from foot machines that required great strength. Men weaving was still rare in the south of the Yangtze River[79] because of high opportunity cost. Suppose a man did not have land in the flourishing age of the Qing Dynasty, if he worked outside, the net income he got was 1.94 litres of rice per day after deducting the cost of meals. In contrast, if he

[78]It is mentioned in *Book of Shen* that the wage of a woman was only half of a man in the late Ming Dynasty. Based on the work of Mann, the wage of a woman was only 30% to 60% that of a man in 1930 in the Ningbo area (Mann, 1992). It is calculated by 50% here.

[79]As is recorded in *Chronicles of Shanghai County* in Kangxi Era, most of the folk men were idle whereas women were laborious. They tended to weave all day and night and supported themselves. According to *Chronicles of Shanghai County* in Qianlong Era, in the low season, as much as 100,000 of cotton could be produced, so the folk men tended to rely on the women to support him. It is clearly seen that a man did not weave in the low season.

was to be engaged in textile, the net income was just 0.9 litre of rice per day after deducting the cost of meals as a result of low production efficiency, which was still less than that of a woman with 1.5 litres of rice.

On the whole, the net income of the cotton textile industry of Songjiang in the Ming and Qing Dynasties was far above that of agriculture. According to historical records, the profit of the textile industry was higher than that of the planting industry,[80] and thus almost all the women were willing to work in the textile industry instead of in agriculture. Compared with the traditional pattern of "men tilling the farm and women weaving", the work division of this new-type industry was quite different. Women of Songjiang were engaged in large-scale commercial activities with the purpose of "produce for market". The prosperity of the cotton textile industry in Songjiang can be attributed to the rural women's pursuit of profit, but not to make a living.

Besides, we have to realize that the prosperity of the handicraft industry in rural areas was not only different from the weaving area in the Republican period described in the third chapter, but also from the industrialization of the Western Europe period. Hence it is hard to take it as "proto-industrialization". In the Ming and Qing Dynasties, the characteristic of rural industrialization was that the cotton textile industry was popular and profitable. However, the male laborers were not attracted, and the traditional pattern of men–women division was not broken. Therefore, the cotton textile industry of the south in Ming and Qing Dynasties was neither so-called "involution" nor "proto-industrialization" of Western Europe, but a kind of "female industrialization" without male labor. The cotton textile industry has 200 years of history, but why did "proto-industrialization" of Western Europe not exist in the cotton textile industry? This question will be discussed in the following chapter. Now let us discuss the development of female industrialization at the end of the Qing Dynasty and the Republican period.

The "Sudden" Decline of Songjiang Cotton Textile Industry at the End of the Ming Dynasty and the Beginning of Republic of China

After the First Opium War, the cotton textile industry of Songjiang area was affected by foreign yarn and cloth. The economic penetration

[80] Qianlong, *Chronicles of Qingpu County.*

of foreign capitalism to Chinese economy is one of the most important issues in Chinese modern economic history. Scholars differ in the influence of commercialization to agricultural economy. On the contrary, scholars are in agreement on the influence of commercialization to handicraft industry. The traditional hand-made products compete with foreign and domestic machine-made products, and then die out gradually, though the pace of decline varied from industry to industry. In fact, scholars concerned about the revitalization of the homespun industry under the competition of foreign cloth and domestic machine-made cloth still take a negative attitude toward the future of hand-made cloth (Yan, 1955; Zhao and Chen, 1977; Wu, 1985). In conclusion, the decline of traditional handicraft industry had a negative impact on small farmers and finally agriculture (Huang, 1985).

I do not hold the view that hand-made homespun was superior to foreign cloth and machine-made cloth. Instead, my view is that the hand-made homespun industry did not decline in the face of strong external forces. In fact, it made great changes in the aspects of production, market organization, technical innovation, etc. Actually, the hand-made homespun industry still stayed normal and stable even on the eve of the Anti-Japanese War, and a lot of farmers even benefited from the handicraft industry. What interests me most is the flexible change of traditional handicraft industry faced with the machine-made products and its influence on farmers.

The import of foreign yarn and cloth firstly affected the cotton textile industry of Songjiang. Although many local people insisted on the decline of homespun industry from the middle of the 19th century,[81] the homespun industry of Songjiang kept its prosperity till the First World War. According to Xu Xinwu, in 1860 of the Xianfeng (1850–1861) era, weaving households took up 90% of Songjiang, with an average output of 66 bolts of cloth per household in a year. In other words, 1.5 laborers were needed to work for 265 days in a year. In the 20th century, the homespun industry of Shanghai was still prosperous until the First World War, with 23 million bolts of cloth being sold abroad, which had little decrease compared with that in the 18th and 19th century. However, the homespun industry declined suddenly at the end of the First World War, namely the beginning of the 20th century. There are no specific statistics although, according to some oral materials and historical documents, the cotton textile industry of Shanghai's surrounding

[81] Bao Shichen says "the price of foreign machine-made cloth today is one third of shuttle cloth. In the past, we depend mainly on the weaving industry, but now, there is no yarn to weave, and the cotton is reduced by half in Songjiang and Taicang." It is the situation in 1846, which is recorded in the 26th volume of *Four Aspects of Anwu* written by Baohen.

areas had declined around 1930. Hence cloth-weaving was not a kind of commodity production but the self-use of households.[82]

Most scholars consider the rapid decline of homespun industry in the 1920s to be a result of the growth of foreign and domestic industrial products after the First World War (Yan, 1955; Xu, 1992). However, there are still two questions about this viewpoint.

First, the decline of homespun industry was based on the price competition of foreign cloth and homespun. Specifically, in the 1920s and 1930s, the price of foreign cloth and machine-made cloth reduced continuously, whereas the price of homespun remained unchanged, which made it possible for the homespun industry to lose its competitiveness (Xu, 1992). The price changes of foreign cloth and homespun are shown in Table 4-1.

As shown in Table 4-1, in the 1920s, the price of foreign cloth fell sharply, while the price of homespun remained unchanged and even rose slightly. Therefore, the homespun had lost its competitiveness.

Now one is to find out why the price of homespun remained at such a high level, and whether the price of homespun was close to its cost price and could not be reduced. Let us look at the net income of a bolt of cloth before the decline of homespun.

During the First World War, homespun was replaced by foreign yarn to weave in the Songjiang area. Women generally could weave 1.5 bolts of cloth in a day, and some could even weave 2 bolts. According to some local households, weaving a bolt of cloth could get 2 or 3 *jiao* (1 *jiao* = 0.1 yuan) excluding cost, which amounted to 4 or 5 *jin* of rice,[83] or about 3 litres. Compared to the net income during the Ming and Qing Dynasties, the net income of this time was the highest.[84]

The result makes the decline of homespun industry in the rural Shanghai area even more puzzling. Why did weaving tend to decline if

---

[82]Based on the oral material in *Homespun Industry of South of the Yangtze River*, foreign cloth sold well after 1922, whereas the homespun had become less popular than before. Until 1927, some homespun shops which also sold foreign cloth mainly focused on homespun industry, and some even gave up homespun to sell foreign cloth. Around 1930, the production of homespun was suspended except in four households of Songjiang that weaved for their own use, which led to homespun shops closing or turning to sell foreign cloth (Xu, 1992: 278).

[83]*History of Homespun Industry of South of the Yangtze River*, pp. 242–244.

[84]Deducting a litre of rice eaten by a weaving woman in a day, there were still 3 to 4 litres of rice. There were only 1.15 litres in the late Ming Dynasty, 1.5 litres in the flourishing age of Qing, and at least 0.7 litre during the Jiaqing to Daoguang era.

the net income of weaving was so high? If it is true that homespun was of high price and little competitiveness, which provided for a homespun industry with much reduction space, then why did the price of homespun tend to rise instead of reducing?

The second problem is that the homespun in Shanghai (Songjiang)[85] obviously declined; however, the homespun industry was prosperous in the surrounding areas of Shanghai, especially in Jiangyin, Changshu, Pinghu, Haining and Nantong until 1937 when Japan invaded. The transfer of the homespun area from Songjiang to the surrounding areas suggests that the decline of homespun industry was not just a phenomenon when faced with industrial products. Simultaneously, another question arises, namely, why this geographical change occurred in the homespun area in the 20th century (see Table 4-3).

These two questions are elaborated in the following two parts.

Rural Industrialization in Shanghai

The most important reason for the high price of homespun cloth was the growth of labor opportunity cost in Shanghai instead of the unreasonably low price for farmers. In other words, farmers had to find other opportunities to make more money, and thus they gave up weaving which led to its decline.

As the biggest city in China, Shanghai experienced a rapid rise at the beginning of the 20th century, which had a great influence on rural areas, providing more non-agricultural job opportunities. The rise of Shanghai was the result of commercial intercourse of port and opening up to the outside world. The whole process included two stages: the first stage covered the inflow of foreign capital, the establishment of a chamber of commerce, and the investment in setting factories after the First Opium War; the second stage was the rapid development of national industry and commerce in Shanghai during the First World War. In other words, Shanghai had experienced commercialization first, and then industrialization, which were exogenous to local farmers. The specific influence of commercialization and industrialization to rural economy is as follows.

At first, large numbers of labor were needed during the process of industrialization in Shanghai, which may in turn benefit the rural areas of

[85] Shanghai witnessed a great rising during the First World War. Since the 1920s, the Songjiang area was renamed as Shanghai.

Shanghai. Based on the local chronicles of Shanghai, one can find evidence for the reduction of agricultural labor. In addition, more and more female laborers tended to participate in agricultural production. In Chuansha County, "more and more strong men tend to go to Shanghai to learn doing business, skills, or work in foreign factory. Therefore, women have to do agricultural work. It is quite different from the situation in the past" (Fang and Lu, 1991). It is clear that more and more male labor flowed into Shanghai, and women had to cultivate rural land. Meanwhile, labor exiting agriculture brought about a scarcity of labor, the rapid growth of price and wage of labor. Nanhui County faced a lack of labor. As a result, it was very hard to hire a laborer. "After breakfast, they go to work in the farm. Then they stop working and have lunch, and the employer prepares them for five pieces of pork, which is called 'Meihua pork', which is the superior pork, together with vegetables. The dessert is also prepared for them in the afternoon, and they finish their work in an early time. Wine, fish, egg, etc. are provided for supper, they all tend to leave until they get drunk. During working hours, laborers tend to smoke as much as eight times, and they only work less than three hours a day; in rainy season, the wage is as high as 300 pennies a day, so more and more people are willing to work, even the small children" (Yan and Liu, 1991).

In addition, a lot of female labor flowed into Shanghai and worked in factories. According to the records of Qingpu County, many rural women gave up weaving and went to work in Shanghai. "Women in rural areas not only help their family to cultivate, but also weave. Since the middle of Guangxu (1874–1908) era (after 1900), this custom changes gradually, woman picks up the bad habits in the city and starts to dress them up just like the city woman. Therefore, woman has to make a living and work in other places, especially in Shanghai because of high wage" (Yu *et al.*, 1991). Rural women gave up weaving not because of the low income, but because they were affected by the bad habits in the city and wanted to search for a job of higher wage. Moreover, many factories were established in rural areas of Shanghai, which provided women with more job opportunities, especially in Shanghai County. According to *Chronicles of Shanghai County* in the Republican period, most women worked in the factories in rural northeast areas (Wu *et al.*, 1991). In Chuansha County, women gave up weaving and worked in factories producing towels, leading to the rapid development of the factory in the early 20th century. On the eve of the Japanese War of Aggression, the number of the towel factories in the county reached 202, with 8,695 employees, accounting for one-fifth of women in the whole county.

Table 4-4 Percentage of Labor Engaged in Non-agricultural Work in Total Amount of Labor Forces in Chuansha County

	Male	Female	Total
Total population	72,149	70,402	142,651
Labor	48,742	45,186	939,928
Work outside (n=) (%)	21,373 (43.8%)	5,954 (13.2%)	27,327 (29.1%)
Work in towel factory (n=) (%)	—	1,656 (3.7%)	
Work in lace industry (n=) (%)	—	23,050 (51.0%)	

If women could not go to Shanghai or work in factories,[86] there were still some other jobs with high wage. One was the lace industry which arose in the First World War. It was organized by merchants, and raw material was provided in rural areas. The merchant would show the laborers a specific style, buy the products and then pay for processing charges. Knitting in Shanghai County, as well as lace in Chuansha and Nanhui County were very popular at that time. Since the establishment of towel factories in Jiading County, the putting-out system was adopted, "towel machines are indispensable and exist in every household. Some have at least one or two and some even have six to seven" (Pan and Wang, 1999). Besides, some similar industries also existed in Songjiang County and Chongming County.

Let us take the situation of Chuansha County as an example, and the statistics of inflow labor, the number working in factories and engaging in the handicraft industry are all shown in Table 4-4.

The demographic date in the table (population, labor and rural migration numbers) is based on the census of Chuansha County in 1935. The data of towel factory and lace industry are based on the survey of towel industry and lace industry in 1930 (Fang and Lu, 1991).

As shown in Table 4-4, it is clear that nearly half of the men of Chuansha County were engaged in non-rural industry, whereas only 13% of women tended to work in non-rural industry; however, most of the local women were engaged in handicraft industry. Is it true that the wages of the lace industry was much higher than that of agriculture?

According to *Chronicles of Chuansha County*, "these thirteen or fourteen years old girls who are engaged in lace industry can gain three

[86]Influenced by traditional thought, people in rural areas were concerned about the gender factor and misgoverned management system, so they were not willing to work in the factory except for those who had to work in the factory to support their family (See oral material of people surnamed Xue and Zhang of Sanlintang (Xu, 1992)).

or four *jiao* per day", "during the prosperous period, the wage is as high as million yuan each year, and the wage of women varies from two or three jiao to four or five" (Fang and Lu, 1991). It was equivalent to 7.8 *jin*, or 5 litres of rice, which amounts to 4 litres after deducting 1 litre of rice for own consumption, which is twice as much as the net income of weaving.

In addition, there are no other statistical data about the income of the handicraft industry, while written materials are abundant. For instance, according to the people who were engaged in cloth-weaving in Jiangwan of Shanghai County, they obtained the wool materials from shop owners of Jiangwan County, and the income they got by processing the finished product was higher than that of cloth-weaving. Therefore, more and more people tended to knit wool. After the Battle of Shanghai on January 28, 1932, Gaojing Temple of Jiangwan County was destroyed, and the production process ceased. Therefore, many people turned to wool-knitting and vegetable production. "Around 1920, with the development of subsidiary businesses such as lace-making, mesh bag-knitting and wool-knitting in Xinzhuang of Chuansha County, much working time was saved and high wage was provided for the people, and thus some young girls did subsidiary business instead of weaving. In the year of 1930, most people were engaged in subsidiary businesses such as making lace, knitting mesh bags, and agricultural production except some old people who were still engaged in the textile industry" (Xu, 1992: 303–305).

On the whole, the decline of the cotton textile industry with 300 or 400 years of history did not mean the decline or even involution of rural economy. On the contrary, it was the result of farmers looking for a better job opportunity. In terms of cotton textile industry, it is still hard to assert that the decline of hand-weaving was because of the change of the national hand-weaving industry center. In fact, the production center of homespun was changed from Shanghai to the surrounding regions in the 20th century, even to Nantong and Haimen in the north of the Yangtze River.

Proto-industrialization outside Songjiang Region

The cotton textile industry existed around the Songjiang prefecture in the Ming and Qing Dynasties but did not reach its heyday. In the middle of Qing, cotton cloth was made in Changshu, Wuxi and so on. The production of cotton cloth in Changshu was 10 million, which amounted to one-third of that in Songjiang prefecture. Most of the products were sold to Jiangsu Province and Zhejiang Province, others were sold to as far as Shandong

Table 4-5 Output of Homespun in Several Weaving Areas in the South of the Yangtze River in the 1920s and 1930s

Province Level	County Level	Annual Output of Homespun (10,000 tons)
Jiangsu	Jiangyin County	1,200–1,300
	Changshu County	1,200–1,500
	Changzhou County	800
	Nantong County	924
Zhejiang	Haining County	250
	Pinghu County	160–200
Total		4,804

Sources: Xu (1992).

and Fujian,[87] which cannot be compared with the homespun of Songjiang, which were sold to the world (Xu and Wu, 1985); besides, the cloth of Wuxi was mainly sold to the north of Jiangsu in the amount of 3 million.[88] This situation lasted until the sudden decline of weaving in the Songjiang region between the end of the 19th century and the beginning of the 20th century.

In the beginning of the 20th century, the homespun industry developed rapidly in the rural areas outside Songjiang prefecture and reached its prosperity in the 1920s and 1930s. Interestingly, all these areas were distributed in the outer areas of the Songjiang region, and these regions and rural areas of Shanghai mutually interacted in the development of the homespun industry. The areas included Jiangyin, Changshu, Changzhou of south Jiangsu, Nantong, Haimen of north Jiangsu, Haining and Pinghu of Zhejiang, which were the surrounding areas of Shanghai. The output of homespun in these areas in the 1920s and 1930s is shown in Table 4-5.

As the table shows, the total output of a few big cloth-weaving regions in Songjiang exceeded 30 million a year. These were mainly sold to Shanghai first, and then to the whole country. That is to say, the business center of homespun was still in Shanghai, but the production regions were widened. Did the homespun industry of rising areas break the limit of gender division

[87]According to *Yi Ban Lu* (《一斑录》) written by Zheng Guangzu, the value of cotton output in Chang and Zhao Counties was about 5 million, which was sold to Huai, Yang, and Shandong of the north, Zhejiang and Fujian of the south.

[88]As is mentioned in *Xi Jin Shi Xiao Lu* (《锡金识小录》) written by Huang'ang, merchant tended to collect the cloth and transport it to Huai, Yang, Gaoyou and Baodi, with sales of many million *liangs*.

in the cotton textile industry of Songjiang area, and become a proto-industrialization area like the big three cloth-weaving areas of North China? In order to find out the answer to this question, one has to take the production of homespun and its profit into consideration.

Let us take the situation of Jiangyin County and other areas as an example. In the 1920s and 1930s, the homespun industry witnessed a prosperous development, with 100,000 cloth-weaving machines in Jiangyin County. According to the survey, on the eve of the Anti-Japanese War, there were 57,973 picking machines, 30,380 hand machines, 12,680 ironwood machines, totaling 101,033 (Xiao, 1958). This was the situation in 1936. Based on the survey of 1931,[89] the total number of households was 147,100, with 88,200 people. Calculating by the number of farmer households,[90] each household had 1.15 cloth-weaving machines. If the picking machines and hand machines were operated by women, and the ironwood machines were used by men, the women who engaged in cloth-weaving took up 67% of all the female labor, and the men who weaved the cloth accounted for 10% of all the male labor. Compared with the cotton textile industry of Songjiang in the Ming and Qing Dynasties, male labor took part in the homespun industry of Jiangyin, but only a limited number of males were engaged, which was far fewer than those in the rising homespun industry of North China.

Now let us take the net income of weaving into consideration.

The picking machine was used to weave the "small homespun" or "large pieces of cloth" of Jiangyin. Under the putting-out system, the wage per day of these two kinds of cloth was almost the same. That is, "one bundle of yarn and two bushels of rice". A bundle of yarn could be used to weave 10 bolts of cloth, and a bolt of cloth was made in one day. Together with the surplus yarn, it amounted to 3 litres of rice. In this way, the wage of a woman was about 2.3 litres of rice per day; the net income was 2 litres after deducting rice for own consumption, namely, 3 *jin* of rice. If the foot machine (ironwood machine) was used, the wage per day should be 4.5 litres of rice. If male labor was used, the net income was 3 litres of rice after deducting grain ration for personal consumption, amounting to 4.5 *jin*

[89] The data are based on material of 1931 in *Statistical Abstract of the Republic of China* (《中华民国统计提要：廿四辑》). In addition, there is the number of households and population recorded in *Chinese Industry: Jiangsu Province* (《中国实业志：江苏省》) (1933) and *Statistical Abstract of the Republic of China* (1934). But due to the lack of the number of farmer households, I use the data of 1931.

[90] The industrial and commercial units cannot be taken into consideration because the homespun industry was mainly undertaken by farmer households.

Table 4-6 The Average Daily Net Income of a Weaver in Several Weaving Areas (Calculated by Litre of Rice)

	Wages (under pick loom, female)	Agricultural workers (male)
Jiangyin county	2.3	1.5
Changshu county	2.3	3.3
Changzhou county	2.3	2.0
Nantong county	5.0	3.0
Haining county	2.4	—
Pinghu county	2.2	—

The wages of agricultural Changgong in Nantong are calculated according to the average wages of those of Nantong county and Haimen county because both counties were weaving areas in Nantong city and the wages of the weaver were also the average of the two (Ministry of Industry Bureau of Trade, 1933; Lin, 1984).

Sources: Xu (1992).

of rice. If one is to compare the profit with that of homespun in Songjiang area during the same period, one will find that the net income per day was very similar, with 3 to 4 *jin* of rice. However, the people of Songjiang gave up weaving, whereas the people of Jiangyin were willing to do it.

We can also find out that the reason why the weaving region was changed from Shanghai to the surrounding regions, was that farmers requested for it as wages were low as the profit of textile industry was much higher than that of agriculture.

Based on the statistical data around 1930, the wages of long-term male laborers in Jiangyin County was 40 yuan, amounting to 4 *dan* of rice, with the net income of 1.1 litres of rice per day. It is thus obvious that the net income of weaving exceeded that of agriculture at that time, which was also an important reason male laborers began to be engaged in textile industry.

Based on the previous data, the net income of several new weaving regions in the south of the Yangtze River is shown in Table 4-6.

The table shows that the wage of some weaving regions in the south of the Yangtze River reached 2.3 litres of rice per day, totaling 3.5 *jin* of rice. As mentioned previously, the wage in Shanghai was about 3 litres of rice in the same period, 25% higher than that of the south of the Yangtze River. Therefore, in terms of the homespun businessmen, it was more appropriate for them to do homespun business in the south of the Yangtze River than in Shanghai because it could save 25% of labor costs.[91]

[91]The oral materials show that the reason for the outward-transferring of homespun in Shanghai was the difference in labor cost. "At that time, the homespun industry in

Compared with agriculture, the homespun industry was still profitable. As shown in Table 4-6, the daily wage of weaving was higher than that of agriculture. Therefore, more and more people turned to the homespun industry, and some regions even had the phenomenon of "weaving in abandoned fields, which never happened in the flourishing period of weaving region in Songjiang" (Xu, 1992: 505). If it is difficult for us to regard the Songjiang weaving region of the Ming and Qing Dynasties as "proto-industrialization", there is no doubt that a lot of weaving regions in the south of the Yangtze River in the Republican period had become real "proto-industrialization" areas.

Based on the analysis in this chapter, the phenomenon of involution did not exist in the south of the Yangtze River, taking Songjiang prefecture as the center of the zone in the Ming and Qing Dynasties. During the late Qing Dynasty and early Republican period, there were no trends of involution, but prosperous industrialization in rural areas. Besides, with the development of industrialization in the surrounding areas of Shanghai, the homespun industry began to rise in some rural areas of the Yangtze River Delta.

Shanghai tended to decline without resource. Some homespun shops like Heng Qianren and Yu Yuanmao changed their sites, sold the yarn and collected the cloth from the farmers. The wage in Changshu was lower than that in Shanghai, and the cloth was much longer than that in Changshu, so it was easier to sell the homespun in Shanghai" (Xu, 1992: 512).

Chapter 5

Quantitative Analysis on Institutional Change and Rural Industrialization

In the previous two chapters, we explored the history of cotton textile industry in the North China Plain and Jiangnan Region. We discovered that despite differences in their flourishing levels and development times, cotton textile industry in the rural areas achieved its peak simultaneously after entering the 19th century. During this period, many cloth-spinning areas in both Jiangnan and Jiangbei (north of the Yangtze River) regions had extraordinarily active performance, and showed very similar characteristics of European proto-industrialization prior to the Industrial Revolution, such as the interference of labor forces, the prevailing of the putting-out system, and the improving of income from spinning, etc. This chapter will analyze these cloth-spinning regions. The problem to be solved is very simple and clear: why did cloth-spinning regions appear in these regions? What made the rural industry in one region more flourishing than another?

In the literature review of Chapter 2, we specially discussed at length the research concerning the regional distribution of rural industrialization. We found that the biggest deficiency in these research is that there are many individual case studies but barely any analysis on the cross-regional numbers. As a result, when regional studies are different, the same factor may have an opposite effect. For example, dispersion of landholding and fragmentation are considered to be good for developing the rural industry while in other regions, scholars may find that concentration of landholdings was also favorable for proto-industrialization.

This chapter contains a series of empirical research hypothesis to find out the factors determining the rural industrialization in a region and their importance. However, the empirical materials in this chapter come from China of the 20th century. As mentioned previously, China in this period also had flourishing rural industrialization and when one tries to find out its flourishing factors, what one uses is exactly the European experience.

Historical Data

According to the analysis conducted in the previous chapters, one already established that, after entering the 20th century, a relatively flourishing rural cotton textile industry appeared in the rural areas in North China and the Jiangnan Region. Among them, some regions produced solely for commodity production and sale, resulting in higher income than the rural pro-industrial regions. Here, I will try to analyze and find the main factors that promoted the boom of cotton textile industry of a region based on the county-level data.

These data mainly come from the statistical materials of the General Post Office of the Republic of China during 1934–1935. This historical material is mainly about the annual performance of export sales and outbound freight in the entire county collected by staff in all the country-level post offices throughout the country, including the price, total amount and destination of all kinds of local handicrafts. Since this was a special product investigation launched by the General Post Office instead of a conventional one, these data include not merely the products consigned for shipment but also the investigation result made by staff when investigating the local market, including name, industry involved and location of all the important firms in the entire county. One can assume that product data mostly came from investigation of all the firms. Through these data, one can calculate precisely the annual export sale of each county in China. Since the most developed region of cotton textile industry was concentrated in three provinces in North China, Jiangsu Province and Zhejiang Province, the materials used include the export sale data of handicrafts in the 478 counties of the five Eastern provinces.

As for other materials in each county of the five provinces, such as population, land, transportation, historical background and the producing organization of the handicraft industry, I obtain them through referring to all kinds of fragmented historical statistical materials, economic history and local logs.

Table 5-1 Basic Information on Counties in Five Eastern Provinces in China

	Province	Number of Counties	Total Population	Total Household	Population Density	Total Peasants	Average Land Held by Household (*mu*)	Percentage of Yeoman (%)
North China	Hebei	128	219,568	38,711	262	33,027	23.4	69.9
	Shandong	107	342,700	62,264	303	55,314	19	65.9
	Henan	107	310,296	54,514	260	45,662	22	56.3
	Average		286,477	51,024	275	43,953	21.6	64.4
Jiangsu and Zhejiang	Jiangsu	61	533,134	105,886	347	82,898	18.3	38.3
	Zhejiang	75	264,258	61,257	220	42,204	13	27.1
	Average		384,857	81,218	276	45,245	15.4	32.1

The basic information of the five provinces is shown in Table 5-1. Since the three provinces in North China and Jiangsu Province and Zhejiang Province belonged to two different economic regions, I have listed their natural and economic information in the table. The table shows that the difference between the two regions was big while that among provinces of the two regions was relatively small. The total population of each county in North China was smaller than that in Jiangzhe Region (Jiangsu and Zhejiang Provinces). In other words, the scale of county in North China was smaller than that in the Jiangzhe Region. As for population density, Jiangsu Province was the highest, followed by Shandong Province and the other three provinces sharing little difference. In terms of the average land area owned by every peasant household, that in Jiangzhe Region was obviously smaller than that in North China, with 15.4 *mu* (1 *mu* = 0.0667 hectares) and 21.6 *mu* respectively. A more obvious difference can be found in the land tenancy system of the two regions. In North China, the number of yeomen took up more than half of the total peasant household while in the Jiangsu and Zhejiang Provinces, the ratios were 38.3% and 27.1%, respectively. I will divide the five provinces into two economic regions and investigate them respectively in the analysis of this chapter.

Determinants in the Rural Homespun Cloth Industry

According to the research by European scholars, the factors affecting the rural cotton textile industry in a region include population density, the development of commercial agriculture, land institution and transportation. In the following, let us discuss these factors.

Population Density

The relation between population and economy is relatively complex. Seen from the long-term trends in history, they affect each other mutually. The consensus reached by many scholars is that economic development promotes the growth in population and the pressure brought by population growth will in turn slacken economic growth and even hamper its development. But such pressure has two sides to it. Recently, some scholars have contended in their research that a large population is a determinant to technological advancement, and a larger population is favorable to form effects of scale and professional labor division, thus promoting economic growth (Kremer, 1993; Johnson, 1999). Here, I will verify the influence cast by population on the development of the rural handicraft industry.

In the long run, economic development also has obvious influence on population change. As mentioned earlier, Mendels has found that proto-industrialization can promote early marriage, which has obvious influence on population growth. Thus, it is hard to determine the relation between rural industrialization and population growth. This was the case in Europe. But in China, especially in the Republic of China, their relation was very obvious.

In the 1970s, some demographers in Princeton University used new statistical technology to re-analyze the data obtained by John Lossing Buck in rural areas of China during the 1920s and 1930s. The result shows that the population in the Republic of China stopped growing in an obvious way at the end of the Qing Dynasty and at the beginning of the Republic of China after rapid growth in the Qing Dynasty (Barclay *et al.*, 1976). Little change in population in most regions throughout the country has been found for decades. This discovery clearly shows that instead of considering the population change caused by economic growth in the short-term, one can assume that the spatial distribution of population density had an influence on the regional distribution of the handicraft industry. Hence, the population density of a region is considered as an exogenous variable in quantitative analysis.

Agricultural Development

The level of agricultural development has always been regarded by scholars as the most important factor affecting the non-agricultural development in a region. It is mainly affected by the pressure of land imposed by population and the development of commercial agriculture. To many scholars, population pressure was the most important factor leading to agricultural stagnancy since the Ming and Qing Dynasties. In modern times, population pressure, together with commercialization, led to the agricultural "involution", making the agriculture in China border on merely eking out a living (Elvin, 1973; Huang, 1985). In addition, commercial agriculture has made progress since the Song Dynasty and achieved a boom until the Ming and Qing Dynasties and the Republic of China. Although it is studied by many scholars, the discussion about the influence of this commercial agriculture imposed on rural industrialization is not sufficient (Gao, 1995; Zhang, 1997). In the following analysis, I will put the variables concerning both measuring the population pressure in a region and the developing level of commercial agriculture into the analysis framework.

I will use arable land per household to measure the population pressure[92] while the development of commercial agriculture will be measured by the average ratio of the cotton land to the total arable land in the entire county. The less the arable land per household, the more possible that the agriculture in this region bordered on merely eking out a living; and the more the arable land per household, the more likely to develop commercial agriculture. However, it is hard to determine the developing level of agriculture by merely assessing arable fields per household. For example, the Yangtze Delta Region had the smallest area of arable land per household, but one knows from the analysis in the previous chapter that the agriculture in this region did not border on merely eking out a living. One should also take the developing level of commercial agriculture into consideration, which will be measured with the ratio of cotton land to the total arable land. In the 1930s, the five provinces in the east mentioned earlier were the most important cotton-growing regions, and in addition, cotton was also the most important kind of crop for commercial purpose in these five provinces[93]; to almost all regions, cotton was purely a commercial crop, for the homespun cloth industry in the east had disappeared after entering the Republic of China; even if cloth was spun for peasant household use, they used foreign yarn to make cloth, with cotton turned into yarn and sold to non-peasants (Xu and Wu, 1990).

Therefore, the developing level of agriculture can be measured using the two variables. If a region had small arable land per household and food crop was the main crop, then the agriculture in this region can basically be defined as agriculture bordering on merely eking out a living. On the contrary, if a region had large arable land per household and cotton-growing areas, then it means that the commercial agriculture in this region was at a high level.

Land Institution

Another major point discussed by scholars is the influence of distribution of land ownership and the land inheritance system on rural industry.

[92]The data of cultivated land and household were taken from the same statistics without the data of population, so it is credible to calculate by each household instead of cultivated land per capita.

[93]Tea planting was more popular than cotton in Zhejiang province. Tea trees mainly grew in hilly areas which may not occupy the growing locations of grain, so cotton was still the most widely planted crop in Zhejiang.

In terms of land inheritance system, there were different systems prevailing in the European countries. But in China, the situation was much simpler. Irrespective of whether in North China or in the Jiangnan Region, the land inheritance system was represented by a uniform equal division to all sons. Since the system had a long history in China and changed little, I do not include it into the analysis model here. But in contrast, the distribution of land ownership differed greatly in different regions. The ratio of yeoman was 60% to 70% in the three provinces in North China; but the situation was different in Jiangsu and Zhejiang Provinces, with the ratio in Jiangsu Province being 38.3%, only half of that in North China and in Zhejiang Province, only 27.1%. In other words, two-thirds of peasants in North China were yeomen while only about one-third of peasants were yeomen in the Jiangzhe Region.

If one looks from the perspective of distribution of labor force and time, the region with more yeomen had greater difficulty in developing the rural handicraft industry. If peasants had part of the land, no matter how much, it would result in opportunity cost when the labor force engaged in other industries. Here, I assume that the ratio of yeomen will have negative influence on the homespun cloth industry: the greater the ratio of yeomen, the less developed the homespun cloth industry.

Transportation

Scholars studying European proto-industrialization point out that the important role played by raw material in the handicraft industry, in fact, refers to the role played by cheap transportation cost in the handicraft industry. In terms of the homespun cloth industry in the Republic of China, whether a place was growing cotton or not was unimportant, for all cloth was spun with foreign yarn instead of homespun yarn made from cotton. In such a case, the transportation in a region was significant to reduce cost of transportation, which included cost resulting from transporting yarn into a place and transporting homespun cloth out of the place. In North China and the Jiangnan Region, there were two means of long-distance transportation. One was transportation by water. In the Jiangnan Region, the river system was very developed and most counties had good transporting advantage; in North China, although there were very few rivers, it was still the most important means of transportation for industrial raw materials and products in the rural area. Even though there were many roads in the northern part, the long journey and heavy load were too much for mules or horses. Besides, the cost was very high. Generally, prosperous towns were located on the riverside. In the heyday of homespun cloth, the Gaoyang cloth region depended on river transport, with most homespun cloth transported along the Zhulong River to Baiyangdian, and then along Daqing River to Tianjin. The homespun cloth in Baodi cloth region was also transported to Tianjin along Jiyun River (Fang and Bi, 1936; Wu, 1936). In China at the turn of the late Qing Dynasty and the early Republic of China, another means of transportation capable of long-distance transportation was railway transportation. Yet railway transportation was a product of the Industrial Revolution. In the following part, I will discuss the completely different factors affecting rural industry in the proto-industrial period in both China and Europe specifically.

Difference of Homespun Industry between China and Europe

When one uses data to verify the research by Western scholars, two extremely important factors should be taken into consideration: the difference in historical background and the market system between China and Europe. The difference is reflected in the following two aspects and one should take them into consideration when verifying the data.

First is the difference in historical background. In Europe, proto-industrialization took place before the Industrial Revolution. But the Chinese proto-industrialization I study here took place after the Industrial Revolution. So it is in fact a "proto-industrialization in the industrial age". At that time, urbanization and industrialization in China were far behind compared with the Western powers. American and European cultures had been introduced to China for almost 100 years. Although changes took place mainly in the city with urban industrialization whereas agricultural labor technology and labor productivity progressed little, improvements took place in the rural market and in transportation (Rawski, 1989). In terms of specific rural communities in a region, exogenous changes were reflected in the appearance of railway and the emergence of neighboring industrial cities. I have summarized them in Table 5-2.

The first railway in China was built after the Second Opium War. By 1935, railway transportation throughout the entire nation was highly developed. Though railway transportation mainly focused on industrial products produced in the urban areas, it also affected rural communities in the proximity as well as those along the track. The areas with railways passing by participate in the market in a deeper way due to

Table 5-2 Information on Whether Counties in the Two Areas Are Near to[94] Railways and Industrial Cities

		North China $n = (\%)$	Jiangsu Province and Zhejiang Province $n = (\%)$	Average of Five Provinces $N = (\%)$
Nearby railway	Y	153 (43.7)	55 (40.1)	208 (42.7)
	N	197 (56.3)	82 (59.9)	279 (57.3)
		350 (100.0)	137 (100.0)	487 (100.0)
Nearby industrial city	Y	21 (6.0)	22 (16.1)	43 (8.8)
	N	329 (94.0)	115 (83.9)	444 (91.2)
		359 (100.0)	137 (100.0)	487 (100.0)

the convenient transportation for agricultural products and quick access to market information (Qian, 1990). For details, see *Pinghan Railroad and Economic Development of Northern China* (Zhang, 1986). By 1936, the railway network in the five Eastern provinces studied had basically formed, with four major railways like Jinpu Railway (Tianjin to Zhenjiang, Jiangsu Province), Pinghan Railway (Beijing to Wuhan, Hubei Province), Jiaoji Railway (Qingdao to Jinan, Shandong Province) and Longhai Railway (Lanzhou, Gansu Province to Lianyungang, Jiangsu Province), and many other branch lines. Table 5-2 shows that 40% of counties in North China and Jiangzhe Region had railways passing through.

After entering the 20th century, industrialization and the machine industry concentrated in some large industrial cities[95] and the handicraft industry was still in a dominant position in the rural areas. These industrial cities included some ancient cities with a long history and large population, such as Beijing, Tianjin, Nanjing and Hangzhou. There were also boom cities that appeared after the opening of treaty ports, such as Shanghai, Qingdao, and Yantai (Shandong Province). Table 5-2 shows that there were about 6% of counties in the three provinces of North China with large industrial cities in their surroundings, and 16% in Jiangsu and Zhejiang Provinces due to the high density of cities. As analyzed in the last chapter, industrial development in these cities had great influence on their surrounding rural areas. It is mainly reflected in the demand for labor force

[94]Near to railways means this county had railways passing through, and near to industrial cities means the county shared borders with the industrial city.

[95]Big cities of east China are Beijing, Tianjin, Jinan, Qingdao, Yantai, Luoyang, Kaifeng, Shanghai, Nanjing, Suzhou and Hangzhou.

from the cities which resulted in labor force from the surrounding rural areas flowing into the cities and increasing the opportunity cost of local labor force. Just like the outward shift of the cloth region in Shanghai, the appearance of industrial cities was expected to impose an opposite effect on homespun cloth, which was produced by cheap labor force. However, bordering cities did no good to the development of the handicraft industry, for there were obvious market opportunities and rich information around the cities.

Since there were no railways and industrial cities before the European Industrial Revolution, the influence of the two factors on rural handicraft industry was not discussed in the existent literature concerning proto-industrialization. But due to the historical background of rural industrialization in the rural areas of China, I will include the two variables in the data analysis.

The difference in the historical background between the Chinese homespun cloth industry and European proto-industrialization may lead to another potential factor. This factor is whether the region had historical records concerning the cotton textile industry, especially in the Qing Dynasty. As mentioned in the previous two chapters, in the Ming Dynasty, there were plenty of areas engaging in the cotton textile industry in North China and the Jiangzhe Region besides some areas in the Songjiang prefecture and Suzhou prefecture. But in these areas, few of the cotton textile industries produced for commercial purpose, with a majority engaging in self-spin and self-use. Here, my hypothesis is this: if a region has historical records concerning the cotton textile industry, it will be easy for it to develop a homespun cloth industry producing mainly for commercial purpose after entering modern times. The reason is very simple: the spinning tradition had trained a group of skilled labor force long engaged in spinning.

In the rural handicraft industry, another aspect with "Chinese characteristics" was the production and market organization of homespun cloth industry. In European proto-industrialization, the putting-out system was a very common organizational form and the activities of putting-out merchants could be found almost everywhere in the flax, wool and cotton textile industries. The organizational form of rural textile handicraft industry in Europe was family-based and organized by putting-out merchants. These merchants distributed materials to peasant households and collected products and paid them in the peasant households after the products were finished. But the case was quite different in China. Prior to the end of the 19th century, although the cotton textile industry in China had reached a very high level (such as in Songjiang prefecture) and enjoyed centurial experience, no record of the putting-out system has been found and peasant households spun and sold cloth on their own (Yan, 1955; Wu, 1983). By the early years of the 20th century, the putting-out system started to emerge with the spread and use of foreign yarn. But obvious differences between different regions can be found. In some regions, the homespun cloth industry was flourishing and there were plenty of putting-out merchants; in some other regions, although the homespun cloth industry was popularized, the cloth was bought by local peddlers and long-distance merchants. In addition, local logs and relevant materials had no record of the putting-out merchants. Take the Dingxian County in Hebei Province as an example. In the 1920s and 1930s, production of homespun cloth in rural areas was widespread in this county. However, peasants generally sold a small amount of cloth they spun to cloth stores in the cities or towns instead of obtaining their payment from putting-out merchants (Zhang, 1991).

I have summarized the information on production and organization of homespun cloth in the counties of the five eastern provinces whose annual productive value surpassed 100,000 yuan[96] in Table 5-3. The table shows that the putting-out system was carried out in about one-fifth of the counties in North China while the ratio was greater in the Jiangzhe

Table 5-3 Distribution of the Putting-out System in Counties (in Which Output Value of Homespun Is over 100,000 Yuan)

	North China	Jiangsu Province and Zhejiang Province	Average of Five Provinces
Having putting-out system	6 (21.4%)	7 (50.0%)	13 (31.0%)
Having no putting-out system	22 (78.6%)	7 (50.0%)	29 (69.0%)
Total	28 (100.0%)	14 (100.0%)	42 (100.0%)

[96] In the counties without homespun industry or with small-scaled homespun industry, the putting-out system was rare. This was the reason why I only investigate the counties with homespun output over 100,000 yuan. What interests me most is that the putting-out system did not exist in all the counties with large-scale homespun industry, so the putting-out system was only one of the decisive factors contributing to the development of the homespun industry. It is clearly shown in Table 5-3 that there are still some other exogenous or endogenous variants besides the putting-out system.

region, with half of the counties producing large amounts of homespun cloth carrying out the putting-out system. Two questions will be answered here. First, to what extent did the emergence of the putting-out system affect the boom of the homespun cloth industry? Second, why did the putting-out system flourish in some areas, but not in others?

The Hypotheses and Test Results of Proto-industrialization

Independent variable (also called explanatory variable) was discussed in the previous two chapters, including demographic factor (population density), agricultural development (cultivated land per household, proportion of cotton field), land system (yeoman proportion), transportation and geographical condition (waterway, railway, and adjacent industrial city), weaving records, and the putting-out system. Besides, I used a dummy variable to control whether there were other handicraft industries except for homespun industry; meanwhile, the sub-variables of province are used in regression as control for the provincial differences. The result is shown in Table 5-4.

As shown earlier, all these variables influence the homespun industry of an area in different aspects, including the influence on labor cost and transaction cost. The results of the influence on labor cost and transaction cost are shown in Table 5-5, serving as the hypotheses.

In Table 5-5, the transaction costs are divided into transportation cost, information cost and coordination cost. The labor cost is not subdivided, including opportunity cost and training cost of labor. As shown earlier, there are five factors affecting the homespun industry. The population density is helpful for the reduction of information cost, technical exchange and quality control in the homespun industry; the waterway and railway transportation not only helped to reduce the transportation cost, but also the information cost; the weaving tradition could reduce the training cost of labor; the putting-out system helped to reduce the transaction cost of the homespun industry which included information cost and coordination cost, because specialized merchants of raw material and product collection appeared so that the exchange of market information became more and more frequent than before. These merchants were much concerned about the type and specification of homespun, and controlled the quality of the homespun though the households tended to weave at home.

The three costs which were not helpful for the development of the homespun industry mainly related to the development level of agriculture. The more cultivated land, the higher the proportion of cotton fields, and

Table 5-4 Descriptive Statistics of Explanatory Variables

		Cases	Average	Reference Point	Min	Max
North China	Population density	328	274.79	139.18	29.47	1,084.78
	Land owned by every household	342	21.56	11.21	2.82	89.34
	The ratio of cotton land	339	0.06	0.13	0.00	0.95
	The ratio of Yeoman	350	64.40	17.84	6.59	100.00
	Waterway transportation	350	0.06	0.23	0.00	1.00
	Railroad transportation	350	0.44	0.50	0.00	1.00
	Weaving tradition	350	0.22	0.42	0.00	1.00
	Nearby cities	350	0.06	0.24	0.00	1.00
	Putting-out system	350	0.05	0.22	0.00	1.00
	The ratio of agricultural population	342	86.65	9.12	52.00	100.00
Jiangsu and Zhejiang Province	Population density	135	276.29	181.03	46.80	1,307.16
	Land owned by every household	136	15.35	7.60	2.65	39.81
	The ratio of cotton land	136	0.07	0.17	0.00	1.00
	The ratio of Yeoman	136	32.10	20.82	4.00	90.50
	Waterway transportation	137	0.33	0.47	0.00	1.00
	Railroad transportation	137	0.40	0.49	0.00	1.00
	Weaving tradition	137	0.15	0.35	0.00	1.00
	Nearby cities	137	0.16	0.37	0.00	1.00
	Putting-out system	137	0.07	0.25	0.00	1.00
	The ratio of agricultural population	136	75.04	13.16	34.00	99.00

the larger the opportunity cost of labor who were engaged in homespun industry. The variable of "adjacent city" had a more complicated influence. If the homespun industry was around the big industrial and commercial cities, making it possible for laborers to go out to work, the opportunity cost was relatively high. However, it was clear that the transaction cost of homespun such as transportation and information cost would be reduced. Hence, the influence of the variable may be positive or negative.

Table 5-5 Effect of Independent Variables on Dependent Variable and the Mechanism (with Hypothesis)

		Transaction Cost			
	Labor Cost	Transportation Cost	Information Cost	Cooperation and Management Cost	The Function of Homespun Industry
Population density			—		+
Land owned by every household	+				—
The ratio of cotton land	+				—
The ratio of Yeoman	+				—
Waterway transportation		—			+
Railroad transportation		—	—		+
Weaving tradition	—				+
Nearby cities	+	—	—		?
Putting-out system			—	—	+

+: increasing or favorable; —: reducing or at disadvantage; ?: not clear.

I take the output per household of a county[97] as the dependent variable, and the distribution (see Table 5-6) is uneven. Among 342 counties of North China and 136 counties of Jiangsu and Zhejiang areas, 79 and 23 counties respectively produced homespun, about one-fifth of the counties. Among the counties producing homespun, the output per household of North China was 24.58 yuan, 41.54 yuan for Jiangsu and Zhejiang. Counties differed greatly in output, of which the highest was Weixian County, in Shandong Province, with an annual output per household of 1,068 yuan, whereas the output per household of some areas was less than 1 yuan. Based on the characteristic of the dependent variable, I will adopt Tobit (sample selecting

[97]Reasons for calculating by the output per household instead of output per capita are as follows: first, the homespun industry was scattered household production, every person in a household tended to work and had clear division of labor (Shi, 1993). The output per household took a household as the production site; besides, the existing household numbers were more persuasive than population.

Table 5-6 Distribution of Homespun Industry Output Value in North China and Jiangsu Province and Zhejiang Province

	North China	Jiangsu Province and Zhejiang Province
Total number of counties	342	136
The number and percentage of counties having homespun industry ($n =$)(%)	79 (23.1)	23 (16.9)
Average output value of each household in counties having homespun industry (yuan)	24.58	41.54
Standard deviation of average output value of household making homespun (yuan)	125.91	106.14

model) to make a regression analysis[98] (Manning *et al.*, 1987). Since the situation was different in North China and the Jiangsu and Zhejiang areas, I will make the regression analysis of these two areas respectively. The results are shown in Table 5-7.

As shown in Table 5-7, the influence of many factors is not obvious. There were only three factors contributing to the development of the homespun industry: population density, weaving tradition and the putting-out system. Let us look at the characteristics of the three factors first.

The population density had a positive impact on the homespun industry both in North China and the Jiangsu and Zhejiang areas. It is to be noted that they were not a linear correlation but logarithmic relation.[99] When the population density increased from the bottom, the influence was apparent. As the population density reached a certain degree, the influence was not that obvious. According to the research, the cotton textile industry was less developed in some sparsely populated areas such as west Zhejiang Province and south Shandong Province, but prosperous in densely populated areas including the middle of Hebei Province, west and north of Shandong Province, and south Jiangsu Province. The bigger the population, the more frequent the knowledge and technical exchange will be, especially information related to the market, which was quite important for commodity production. However, if the population density reached a

[98]In terms of these variables, namely, there was no meaning of dependent variable above below some fixed value (such as zero), Tobit regression analysis is made to modify the influence of the value on variable distribution. In terms of the dependent variable frequently with the value of zero, two-part regression can be used (Manning, *et al.*, 1987).
[99]According to the results, when other variables are controlled, the output per household: Value $= \beta$. ln (Pop-dns) +f (Other-variables).

Table 5-7 Determined Factors of Average Output Value of Each Household Making Homespun

	North China		Jiangsu Province and Zhejiang Province		North China (density of towns as instrumental variable)	
	Coef.	t	Coef.	t	Coef.	p
Population density	3.415	1.693	29.691	2.985	3.587	0.209
Land owned by every household	−0.015	−0.167	0.598	1.204	−0.043	0.744
The ratio of cotton land	3.724	0.563	−13.344	0.61	3.236	0.238
The ratio of Yeoman	−0.047	−0.805	0.024	0.16	−0.064	0.439
Waterway transportation	1.226	0.3	5.409	0.833	3.993	0.465
Railroad transportation	1.890	0.944	0.017	0.002	2.556	0.353
Weaving tradition	7.746	3.608	−22.723	−2.083	10.813	0.000
Nearby cities	1.865	0.473	10.331	1.252	3.212	0.553
Putting-out system	14.878	3.983	49.965	4.229	19.174	0.000
Other handicraft industries	−2.180	−1.119	−1.444	−0.231	−2.276	0.402
Hebei Province	5.850	2.267	6.789	0.056		
Shandong Province	−0.992	−0.378	−1.606	0.659		
Jiangsu Province			−5.645	−0.721		
Constant	−30.438	−2.605	−199.41	−3.168	−36.654	0.023
Number of cases	325		135		325	
Prob > Chi2	0.000		0.000		0.000	
Total regression coefficient	0.082		0.199		0.076	

certain degree, the marginal utility would be diminished, so the influence of population density on homespun is logarithmic.

The influence of the weaving tradition on North China and Jiangsu and Zhejiang areas was just the reverse. In North China, the weaving tradition was recorded in history. Hence it was obvious to promote the development of homespun in the area, because weaving technology and labor could be guaranteed. Why was the influence of the weaving tradition on Jiangsu and Zhejiang areas to the contrary?

Based on the historical background of the weaving areas in the south of the Yangtze River, this phenomenon was easy to understand. The traditional weaving areas in Jiangsu and Zhejiang mainly centered on Songjiang and Suzhou. However, the weaving area was changed with the rapid development of Shanghai and the decline of the local homespun industry in the late Qing Dynasty and the early Republic of China. The rising areas such as Nantong and Haimen of north Suzhou, did not have the weaving tradition. This was the reason why the homespun industry was away from traditional weaving areas. It is shown that the weaving tradition provided homespun production with labor and technology. Once the labor cost rose (as shown in the previous chapter), the homespun area would be changed. Therefore, low labor cost was another indispensable factor for the rise of the homespun industry. In contrast, why did the homespun industry only develop in several areas though there were a lot of areas in North China and the Jiangsu and Zhejiang areas which had large population and low labor cost? Now let us look at the third factor — institutional change.

Table 5-7 indicates that the rise of the putting-out system was the most important factor contributing to the development of the homespun industry. If this system emerged, the output per household would be increased by 15 yuan in North China, and 50 yuan in Jiangsu and Zhejiang areas. There was still an important question: was the putting-out system an endogenous variable or exogenous variable for the homespun industry of an area? If the prosperity of the homespun industry in turn led to the putting-out system, the results of regression analysis are unfounded.

The Endogeneity Problem of the Putting-out System

Two methods will be used to solve the problem. The first is to use historical data to find out the truth, and then to prove it theoretically by using the statistical method. I read some historical literature about the weaving area of North China; I find the weaving tradition existed in Baodi, Gaoyang and Weixian only before the occurrence of the putting-out system. At that time, the homespun industry was not prosperous; weaving was only for their own use, which was similar to the traditional cotton textile industry in other areas. According to the historical data, the homespun industry of Gaoyang started to develop after merchants introduced the iron-wheel machine, and the popularity of the iron-wheel machine depended on the putting-out system. The local merchants of Gaoyang in the late Qing Dynasty bought the wooden-wheel machine (shuffle machine) from Tianjin, and then introduced the iron-wheel machine. The most important was that

> "at first, the merchants work together to explore the machine and adopt the method for subsidy, then extend the industry without much fund, and farmer can make a living without the capital. All the gentlemen and merchants should be advocated to organize and produce wheel machine and thread. Each household should get thread by *jin*, deliver the cloth by *jin* and earn the wage by market price. The poor households can weave without the capital, and the merchants can collect the cloth and have the vendor. Therefore, merchants and households are integrated. This atmosphere is widely spread which largely

inspires all the local people. Several years later, the homespun industry becomes prosperous." (Tianjin Archives, 1989: 227)[100]

"Get the thread by *jin*", "deliver the cloth by *jin*" and "take the wage by market price" are a reflection of the putting-out system. Based on the literary records, the putting-out system promoted the popularity of the iron-wheel machine, but not the prosperity of the iron-wheel machine. The homespun industry led to the emergence of the putting-out system. Each iron-wheel machine cost 50 or 60 yuan, much higher than the net income a year of an ordinary household, and thus a poor household could not afford it.[101] So the application of foreign yarn and the emergence of the iron-wheel machine were the necessary but not sufficient conditions of the prosperity of the homespun industry. To form a large-scale and universal-type commodity production, the corresponding institutional innovation was of great importance.

Besides Gaoyang County, the second-largest weaving area at that time — Weixian County of Shandong Province also had a similar historical record. Indeed, one can only know the situation of certain areas through historical data; one still has to use some materials to make clear the relationship between these two factors.

I chose the town density of a county as an instrumental variable to test the relationship between these two factors.[102] The town density of a county equals to the total number of counties divided by the gross area of the county.[103] In general, the formation of the county was the product of history, which represented the commodity exchange center of an area, with their own distribution regularities. For the rising homespun industry in the early 20th century, town density was undoubtedly an exogenous variable. It would not affect the homespun industry, but had an impact on the development of the putting-out system. According to the survey, a lot of industry existed in rural areas with inconvenient transportation and low density, for example,

[100] This is a part of referendum giving to the department for farm, industry and commerce by Han Weiqing, the general manager of Gaoyang business branch.

[101] The measures of the putting-out system in solving financial matters will be discussed in the following chapter.

[102] According to Hausman (1987), the characteristic of instrumental variable is: it affects the putting-out system (A), but it does not affect the output per household of homespun (B). If we put the variable into the model, the causal relationship tends to be weak, so the relation of A and B is false, and the converse is true.

[103] Because of the limited data, I adopt the density index here (based on actual density, cases should be divided into four types from the bottom to the top, then divided by the highest level of the density).

the largest rural handicraft center in Henan Province — Zhenping County was located in hilly areas of western Henan Province. But for the putting-out system, town density was an indispensable factor.

Compared with the factory system, the production site of the putting-out system was mainly in households. Therefore, the exchange of raw material and cost had an obvious limit on transportation cost — merchants and households had to walk through households and stores. Moreover, there were two indispensable factors of transportation cost: one was the road condition,[104] and the other was town density. The merchants' stores were mainly located in town. Therefore, if the town density of an area was higher, the actual distance between the merchant and a household was relatively shorter, and thus the transportation cost was lower. Based on the survey, the influence of town density on the putting-out system was quite obvious, but not on the output of homespun industry.[105] In order to analyze the appropriateness of the variable, I start with the test of Hausman–Wu. The result is that the coefficient of this variable to the residual term of the output is 0.0013; chi-square value is 0.598, $p \geq 0.1$, so the variable turns out to be appropriate.

I did a regression analysis of the variable in Tobit and the results are shown in the fifth and sixth columns of Table 5-7. There is no obvious change in the result. Still, the putting-out system affected the output of the handicraft industry. The only difference is the influence of population density is not obvious, because population density is correlated with town density.

As shown in Table 5-7, it is strange that the influence of the factors proposed by European scholars are not apparent except population density. So it is not clear whether these factors are important in rural industrialization in China. As a matter of fact, a new variable is added in regression analysis — the putting-out system. It is endogenous compared with other factors though one can see a significant impact of the system on the homespun industry in rural areas. Meanwhile, other exogenous variables may not affect rural industrialization directly, but affect institutional change such

[104]Some scholars even think that the improvement of road conditions in Europe was the basis of the popularity of the putting-out system (Szostak, 1989).

[105]Data about the town density in Jiangsu and Zhejiang areas are limited, so the result only applies to the north of China. After controlling other variables, the regression coefficient of town density to the output of homespun is 2.328 ($T = 0.621$), which is not significant, whereas the coefficient of the putting-out system is 2.458 ($z = 1.881$, $p < 0.1$), which shows significant influence.

as the putting-out system. In other words, these exogenous variables were likely to affect rural industrialization by affecting institutional change (see Table 5-1).

But was this really the case? Let us analyze the factors contributing to the system formation and institutional change.

The Driving Force of Institutional Change

Some factors are discussed in promoting the development of the homespun industry, among which the putting-out system matters the most. As a production and market system, how did it come into being? What was the indispensable factor? In other words, we attempted to discuss the influence of institutional change on non-agricultural development in the previous chapter, and we will analyze why institutional change only took place in these areas instead of other areas.

According to new institutional economists, there are many kinds of factors affecting institutional change: one is the influence of population change, which may put pressure on institutional change, and the other is natural resources and the distribution characteristics of certain resources, which are specific systems formed under specific non-environments. The last is the system formed by history (formal and informal), and the influence of political factors and ideology. Based on the existing theoretical framework, I will try to analyze the factors contributing to the emergence of the putting-out system.

The population factor is measured by population density, which was discussed in the previous chapter. The resource condition is measured by several variables. One is the cultivated land per household, representing the basic resource condition of an area. The other is transportation condition, including railway transportation and waterway transportation. Strictly speaking, the transportation condition of an area belonged to the resource state. Railway transportation was not only the result of economic development of a country, but also the exogenous variable of a county.

Two variables are used to measure the historical and institutional factors respectively. One is the cotton textile industry, and the other is the degree of development of yeoman system. These factors are also discussed in the previous section.

According to the record, the putting-out system in many areas was formed by local gentlemen, merchants and landlords. Hence, they had the capital and awareness for developing a landlord economy. In order to analyze the influence of ideology on the formation of the system, the

Table 5-8 Determined Factors of Institutional Change

	North China		Jiangsu Province and Zhejiang Province	
	Coef.	*z*	Coef.	*z*
Population density	1.439	1.942	2.611	1.875
Land owned by every household	−0.069	−1.864	0.016	0.194
Railroad transportation	−0.848	−1.343	0.292	0.266
Waterway transportation	2.260	2.934	2.059	1.724
The ratio of Yeoman	0.064	2.251	0.003	0.138
The ratio of agricultural population	−0.073	−2.038	0.038	0.453
The ratio of cotton land	−6.491	−1.741	1.008	−0.522
Weaving tradition	1.809	2.807	−0.619	
Hebei Province	−1.828	−1.548		
Shandong Province	−0.685	−0.988		
Jiangsu Province			−0.433	−0.357
Constant	−7.66685	−1.551	−22.485	−2.228
Number of cases	325		1,350.006	
Prob > Chi^2	0.000		0.344	
Total regression coefficient (R^2)	0.329			

agricultural population proportion will be used as a variable. The less the population proportion is, the more merchants and landlords there were, which may have a positive influence on the formation of the putting-out system.

I did a logistic regression model,[106] and the results are shown in Table 5-8.

As seen in Table 5-8, the crucial factor of institutional change was simple in the Jiangsu and Zhejiang areas, but more complicated in North China. In the Jiangsu and Zhejiang areas, there were two kinds of factors: population density and transportation condition. In general, the putting-out system was likely to appear in the area with a certain degree of population density and convenient waterway condition (the population density and institutional change are in logarithm relation). In fact, in the Jiangsu and Zhejiang areas, only Taihu areas such as Suzhou, Wuxi, Changzhou areas, Hangzhou, Jiaxing, and Huzhou areas had such dense population and convenient waterway conditions. Hence the putting-out system emerged in these areas.

[106]The town density index is not taken into logistic, because the variable is highly correlated to population density, which may cause a lot of related questions. Besides, the data are limited to the Jiangsu and Zhejiang areas.

The situation in North China was relatively complex. First, the population and resource availability such as being close to water bodies or rivers were important factors of institutional change. As was analyzed earlier, the industrial transportation in rural areas mainly depended on waterways. However, the waterway condition in North China was not as good as that in the Jiangsu and Zhejiang areas. So the waterway condition in North China was more important than that of Jiangsu and Zhejiang areas (z is 2.934, only 1.724 in Jiangsu and Zhejiang areas). The other resource variable is the cultivated land per household, which did not affect the rural homespun output directly (it is not obvious in the last regression model), but affected the institutional change of an area. The less cultivated land a household had, the more likely the putting-out system appeared. In other words, although the cultivated land per household did not directly affect the homespun industry, it indirectly affected rural handicraft industry by affecting the formation of the putting-out system. Therefore, one should supplement the arguments of European scholars; that is, less cultivated land per household cannot promote the development of handicraft industry of an area, at least in China. This function was realized by institutional change.

As for historical and institutional factors, both the traditional weaving areas and the proportion of yeomen had great influence on the formation of the putting-out system. For the record, the variable exerted an influence both on the putting-out system and the output of homespun industry. Hence weaving technology and labor were quite important not only for institutional change but also for the homespun industry. However, as the measuring factor of the land tenure system, the proportion of yeomen only affected the institutional change of North China, namely, the more yeoman farmers there were, the easier the putting-out system appeared. The primary hypothesis is that the homespun industry was less developed in the areas with more yeomen. Since there is a positive correlation between the putting-out system and homespun industry, the result is the opposite of the primary hypothesis. It is related to the special production of the putting-out system and the form of market system. The reasons can be seen as follows.

One is the risk aversion of households. I will try to analyze it in the following chapter. The putting-out system did not need to maintain production, and it could adjust production scale according to the market demand. In the Republican period, the competition in the homespun industry was fierce, for the price of yarn and cloth were changing all the time. What is more, the putting-out system was the leader at the time. Under such circumstance, a merchant was willing to hire farmers who were on call at any moment: they could work immediately in peak season and stop working in low season but still support their family. Compared with a sharecropper, a yeoman was more appropriate. Meanwhile, in terms of household, as a non-agricultural income, the income of weaving was much higher than that of planting, but it was risky. During the prosperous period of homespun industry, they tried their best to work. But once the price of cloth was cheaper than that of rice, what did they do if they did not have land to cultivate? In the 1980s, land was still popular in China, serving as non-agricultural work. There is a study showing that farmers kept their land not because they need it to survive, but because they wanted to have some insurance against the risk of working in the city (Kung and Liu, 1999).

The other reason is seen in the literature of European economic history. It was found that the landlords always impeded the entrance of non-rural industry which competed for labor together with the landlords. Frankly speaking, I do not have any specific empirical data to illustrate how landlords impeded the merchants from entering. Therefore, the analysis result here is only for reference. In other words, it is obvious that the proportion of yeomen was low in the area with strong landlords, which corroborates with David Levine's result.

On the whole, the relationship between the variables can be demonstrated in Table 5-2. Some exogenous variables such as resource conditions have an indirect influence on the development of rural industry by affecting institutional change, namely the development of the putting-out system. As an exogenous variable, technology innovation had an obvious effect on both the putting-out system and the homespun industry. Although the variable was not added to the model, technological change especially the introduction of the iron-wheel machine and foreign yarn largely affected the putting-out system as shown in literary data. If one takes transportation as one of the variables of technology innovation, the effect will be shown clearly in the model.

The research of European scholars was tested in China, such as population density. Most factors have an indirect influence on rural industrialization by affecting the institutional change of an area. Institutional change, the formation and development of the putting-out system of an area, turned out to be the most important factor affecting the prosperity of the homespun industry. The formation of the putting-out system depended on the factors such as population, resource condition, the land lease system and the commercialization level of agriculture, which were also found by scholars in Europe. Hence one can see the great influence of institutional innovation and change, as well as the wisdom and insight of new institutional economics. The model demonstrates the standard interpretation of new institutional economics to economic history: resource condition, economic development and the previous institution determined the emergence of the new system, which in turn further promoted the development of the economy.

Chapter 6

The Putting-out System and the Prosperity of Rural Homespun Industry

I explored the reasons how the homespun industry developed and reached its prime using the quantitative method in the previous chapter, demonstrating that as a pattern of industry and market organization, the putting-out system played a decisive role in some cotton textile industry areas. From the perspective of quantitative analysis, the key to whether the weaving industry could develop relied on the existence of the putting-out system. This chapter goes further to answer two questions based on these.

(1) Why was the putting-out system so important? How did it work? The micro-analysis in the previous chapter was not enough because I used data at the county level. In this chapter, I will reveal the specific historical processes and mechanisms by which the putting-out system spurred the development of local cotton textile industry by case study, focusing on the situation in the Gaoyang area[107] — the most developed cloth-making area, combined with the situation of that in North China and south of the Yangtze River. In other words, the previous chapter told us that institution was important and this chapter sets out to tell us why institution was important.

[107] I take Gaoyang area as the subject of research, because lots of research have been made by previous scholars, who may provide us with reference. The most valuable one is the investigation on homespun in Gaoyang in 1935 by Wuzhi and other scholars. It is recorded in *A Study on Weaving Industry in Rural Areas*, published in 1936 by Shanghai Commercial Press, which is also one of the main resources of my research.

(2) How did the putting-out system affect the income distribution of peasants as a form different from family production? Compared with the peasants who used what they produced, were the peasants organized by the putting-out system superior to them?

The Putting-out System and the Capital Limits of Peasants

Only in the previous chapter could I prove the role played by the putting-out system on the prosperity of the homespun industry. As I said before in the introduction chapter, for the phenomenon that the homespun industry survived under competition from machine-made cloth and domestic factory-made cloth, the most powerful explanation focuses on the changes of the raw materials and technology innovation of the homespun industry. Many scholars hold the view that the key to the homespun industry revitalizing depended on the replacement of handicraft yarn by muslin (Xu and Wu, 1993), and the replacement of the pick loom by automatic shuttle looms and iron-wheel machines (Wu, 1936; Yan, 1955). Next I will analyze the complex relationships among muslin, iron-wheel machines and the putting-out system.

The replacement of muslin by handicraft yarn solved two problems in the competition for rural homespun. One was the bottleneck of productivity. If the peasant needed to use handicraft yarn, he needed to spin it. The tool to spin handicraft yarn did not change much since the Yuan, Ming and Qing Dynasties. The spinning wheel with a single shuttle was mainly used.[108] In the Ming Dynasty, the cloth a man weaved for one day used yarn that was spun for five days. In the Qing Dynasty, they made a little progress. But they still needed to spin for more than four days. On the other hand, the productivity of muslin was 44 times that of handicraft yarn (Yan, 1955). Under these circumstances, if homespun continued to be weaved from handicraft yarn, the raw materials would be in shortage compared with muslin. After using muslin, productivity improved greatly with more raw materials provided. Using muslin, a man could weave a bolt or a bolt and a half of cloth under a pick loom. Another was the cost of cloth weaving. The price of handicraft yarn was higher than that of muslin because of low efficiency. But the price of homespun was almost the same as that of machine-made cloth. Thus it would not be cost-efficient if the

[108] The reason why the development of weaving technology was so slow is not the research question of this book. According to Zhaogang, it was due to the single-spindle spinning wheel adapted to the labor arrangements of small-scale peasant economy (Chao, 1972).

Table 6-1 Output of Homespun and Its Value in Hebei Province (1929)

	Number of Counties	Output (bolts)	%	Output Value (yuan)	%
Using muslin	44	14,121,988	55	60,306,619	74.1
Using handicraft yarn	45	11,568,925	45	21,053,978	25.9
Total	89	25,690,923	100	8,130,597	100

22 counties use both handicraft yarn and muslin.
Sources: Li (1934): 42.

peasant bought handicraft yarn to weave. And it was too slow to spin yarn by hand to compete with machine-made cloth. By using muslin to weave cloth, the cost of homespun was reduced.

Judging from the description above, the input of muslin provided a prerequisite but not a sufficient condition to the development of homespun. That was because a large amount of muslin had been imported into China by the end of the 19th century and replaced handicraft yarn rapidly and widely. But the homespun industry could not be revitalized by the mere providing of muslin as raw materials. Let us look at the figures in Table 6-1.

Among the 89 counties in Hebei Province, half of them (44) used muslin entirely, a quarter of them (22) used muslin and handicraft yarn and only another quarter of them (23) used handicraft yarn entirely. The output and value of output in areas using muslin entirely were higher than the rest of the two. However, the output of homespun in the counties using muslin varied.

The output of homespun in Gaodi county was about 1 million and that of Gaoyang county was from 2 million to 3 million between 1929 to 1930, which accounted for one-fifth of the total output of homespun in 44 counties using muslin (the general output was 14 million bolts). By the middle of the 1930s, the area producing homespun was more concentrated. Taking the homespun output of Gaodi County, Gaoyang County accounted for 24.5% of that of the entire province, and the homespun value accounted for 51% of the commercial homespun of the entire province. Although there was no data to show how many counties were using muslin during the middle of the 1930s, one can see that muslin was used more than in 1929. Thus, the revitalization of the homespun industry relied on regional specialization. That the raw material of homespun changed from handicraft yarn to muslin was just a prerequisite to the prosperity of the homespun industry. But as the data showed in the previous chapter, institutional changes played a key role in the prosperity of the regional homespun industry.

Advanced technology is often seen as another important condition that allowed the homespun industry to revitalize. The hand loom changed from under the pick loom to the automatic shuttle loom and iron-wheel machine during the late Qing Dynasty to the Republic of China, and the efficiency of each was higher than the previous one by one time. The iron-wheel machine was especially powerful, as its weaving efficiency was only three times less than that of the spinning wheel using electricity, which reduced the difference between hand-weaving and machine-weaving. More importantly, the weaver could use his hands while driving the loom using his feet, which could broaden the cloth. A wooden loom (under pick loom and automatic shuttle loom) could produce one *jin* (500g) of homespun while an iron-wheel machine could produce eight or nine *jin* (4kg or 4.5kg) of cloth, which was close to the specification of machine-made cloth and was called "imitation machine-made cloth" (Yan, 1955). Undoubtedly, the invention of the iron-wheel machine enhanced the competitive ability of homespun. But it was difficult to spread the advanced technology and make it work in an area to some degree. The widespread use of the automatic shuttle loom especially the iron-wheel machine needed an important precondition, which was the putting-out system.

In areas adopting the putting-out system, the iron-wheel machine was adopted rapidly. In 1908, the iron-wheel machine was introduced to the Gaoyang weaving area. By 1915, all old wooden under pick looms were abandoned. Between 1927–1929, there were about 30,000 iron-wheel machines (Wu, 1936). By the end of the reign of Emperor Guangxu (1874–1908), new forms of looms were widely adopted in the Baodi weaving area, while the Weixian county of Shandong province introduced the iron-wheel machine in early years of Republic of China. Around 1915, there were 500 new looms in the whole county. By the 1930s, there were 50,000 iron-wheel machines. The whole weaving area had almost 100,000 pieces of iron-wheel machines, including those of the near counties (Shi, 1995).

In areas without the putting-out system, the use of the iron-wheel machine was not so popular. Most of them used the iron-wheel machine, under pick loom and automatic shuttle loom together. Table 6-2 takes Dingxian County of Hebei Province as an example and shows the technological advancement of an area with developed homespun industry but without the putting-out system.

One can see that while the number of under pick looms reduced quickly, the number of iron-wheel machines and automatic shuttle looms increased rapidly from 1912 to 1932. The number of iron-wheel machines accounted

Table 6-2 Estimation of Number of Looms in Some Villages in Dingxian County (1912–1932)

Time	Iron-wheel Machine		Automatic Shuttle Loom		Under Pick Loom		Total
1912	—		20	7.14%	260	92.86%	280
1917	—		45	16.67%	225	83.33%	270
1922	15	5.88%	72	28.24%	168	65.88%	255
1927	36	14.63%	84	34.15%	126	51.22%	246
1932	69	28.87%	122	51.05%	48	20.08%	239

Sources: Zhang (1991).

for almost 30% of all looms while the number of automatic shuttle looms accounted for more than half of all looms. The efficiency of the iron-wheel machine was twice that of the automatic shuttle loom. What is more, it could produce imitation machine-made cloth which could sell well. Thus it was obviously advantageous compared with the automatic shuttle loom. But it did not dominate here as it did in the three big weaving areas. The peasants still mainly used the automatic shuttle loom, which implied that institutional changes played a role in the widespread use of advanced technology.

The two key reasons why the iron-wheel machine was widely used in these big weaving areas are as follows.

First of all, the putting-out system solved the problem of capital limits of the peasants. That is, "the poor can weave and spin even they have no money" (Tianjin Municipal Archives, 1989). Whether the weaving household used the iron-wheel machine unanimously was limited by one important factor capital. According to Li Jinzheng, "the price of wooden loom is below 10 yuan, while that of the iron-wheel machine is more than 50 yuan" (Li, 1991). The wooden loom mentioned by Li should be the old-styled under pick loom. In Gaoyang, the price of an iron-wheel machine was 50 yuan (Wu, 1936). Yan Zhongping estimates that the price of an iron-wheel machine in Weixian County of Shandong Province was between 70 yuan and 80 yuan (Peng, 1984). Was it expensive for the peasant?

Let us look at the net income of a peasant household. Table 6-3 shows the figure of the four counties in Zhili in the 1920s.

If one only judges from net income, medium and small yeomen with no more than 25-acre fields could generally afford an automatic shuttle machine, but it was difficult for them to buy an iron-wheel machine. Could a peasant then buy an iron-wheel machine with a loan?

Besides the three big weaving areas, there is no evidence that peasants bought the iron-wheel machine with a loan in other areas. A loan

Table 6-3 Net Income of Household Divided by Area of Land in the Four Counties in Zhili Province (Yuan)

	Having No Land	Under 3 Acres	3–5 Acres	6–10 Acres	11–25 Acres	26–50 Acres	Above 50 Acres
Four counties in Zhili Province	18	14	24	38	71	185	831

Sources: Li (1929).

investigation on 526 households in five villages in Dingxian County where weaving cloth was common in the 1930s showed that the number of loans on "managing agricultural capital" accounted for 31%, 32% and 25%, respectively of the overall number of loans in 1930, 1931 and 1932. Most of these loans investigated were for agriculture, including purchasing livestock, buying land, ransoming land, paying rent, acquiring house, procuring water mill, drilling well, paying wages and buying fertilizer. The loans used on the sideline mainly comprised buying bees, cotton gin, and tools to exact oil (Li, 1935). According to an investigation on loans in six villages in Qinghua Yuan of sub-urban Beijing in 1933, 20 of the total loans were for investment, a percentage of 17.5%. Among the 20 loans, nine were for buying livestock, four for buying land, six for business and one for buying duck eggs. Only the last one can be scantily regarded as sideline investment (Li, 1933). Thus one can infer that buying an iron-wheel machine with a loan was not so common according to the aforementioned materials.

Looms were a fixed investment. The weaving household had to invest money to produce regularly, investing mainly in yarn. Yan Zhongping makes an exact calculation according to the situation of Nantong in 1933. The price of an iron-wheel machine was 46.3 yuan, but a weaving household needed at least 70 yuan to run his business normally (Yan, 1955: 282). The price of an iron-wheel machine in North China was even higher. Roughly, a weaving household needed at least 80 to 90 yuan to make the iron-wheel machine work. This figure was big for normal peasants. Thus one can infer that those who used under pick looms and automatic shuttle looms accounting for half of all looms should be medium and small yeomen. They were limited by money and had to use wooden looms with much lower efficiency.

Things changed after adopting the putting-out system. The putting-out traders handed out raw materials to weaving households. Thus they did not need to buy raw materials. Many traders even "loaned" iron-wheel machines to weaving households. The price of the iron-wheel machine was deducted from the pay for weaving, which made it possible for the widespread use of the iron-wheel machine. Wu Zhi makes it clear in his study about the cloth industry in Gaoyang County:

> "the muslin and iron-wheel machine appears. The iron-wheel machine is powerful and the need of raw materials increases. Few rich peasants can buy raw materials by themselves and sell cloth according to their own plan. To ordinary peasant, they are limited by short of raw materials. They have to resort to businessman and get pay by weaving for them, which are normally called "weaver". And the traders call them "machine user". That is, the putting-out traders hand out the raw materials and collect bolts of cloth." (Wu, 1936: 14).

Besides raw materials, the relatively expensive looms were promoted to the poor weaving households through the putting-out system. In Gaoyang, they adopted the method of "loaning the loom and handing out the raw materials". The usual practice was for the weaving household to pay half the price of the loom first. The rest was paid from the wages earned from weaving (Peng, 1962c, Vol. 2: 412). There are also records that some businessmen rented looms to others in Gaoyang (Yan, 1955: 289). In Weixian County, they adopted the guaranteed mortgage payment of the loom (Wang, 1937). In Baodi weaving area, they utilized the putting-out system initially. The putting-out traders bought the looms and yarns, and then handed them out to households (Su, 1984). These weaving households were mostly sharecroppers who were short of money. Thus the putting-out system developed well (Fang and Bi, 1936).

What is more, using the iron-wheel machine was not only about capital, but also involved the use of labor in a family. Unlike the under pick loom and the automatic shuttle loom, the iron-wheel machine could only be operated by a strong man. Once these medium and small households decided to buy an iron-wheel machine, the status and role of weaving changed completely. It was no longer a sideline for housewives. In this case, everyone in the family would take part in the weaving since one piece of iron-wheel machine needed 2.5 to three laborers. Earnings from weaving were the main source of income for the family. Under this circumstance, agriculture activity was influenced to some degree. If there were no putting-out traders, these medium and small households had to rely on themselves and shoulder risks in the market. What is worse, it was difficult for them to make the production activity go on continuously. Specifically, once the yarn price rose and that of homespun descended, the cloth could not be sold in time. Thus these households did not have enough capital to maintain the running of the iron-wheel machine, which was a waste of equipment and male labor. From this point of view, the employment between putting-out traders and the small weaving

Table 6-4 Basic Information on Weaving Households in Different Income Groups in Gaoyang (1932)

	Average			In Total Net Income	
Income Group (Yuan)	Number of Weaving Households	Number of Looms	Number of Employees	Percentage of Weaving Income (%)	Percentage of Weaving by Households (%)
1–50	95	1.31	0.45	68.43	8.16
50–100	95	1.45	0.61	52.38	18.99
100–150	55	1.65	0.55	51.56	18.78
150–200	34	2.32	1.18	53.76	20.67
200–250	12	2.75	1.50	43.79	38.60
250–300	12	2.67	1.58	36.99	38.33
300–400	17	2.41	1.53	46.08	35.50
400–500	5	2.6	2	0	86.68
500–600	6	2.5	2	6.29	78.52
600–700	6	4	3.50	30.72	49.52
700–800	1	3	0	0	95.88
800–900	11	7	7	100	0
900–1000	1	3	6	91.48	0
1000–1500	2	5.5	6	93.54	3.83
1500–2000	1	9	14	61.16	0
2000–2500	1	5	6	92.02	0

households helped the latter reduce market risks and ensure production went on continuously.

Besides records of cases, systemic statistics about relationships between households and putting-out traders were few and difficult to find. The data on more than 300 weaving households in Gaoyang County obtained by Wu's investigation in 1932 can indirectly show that it was precisely those who had small pieces of land who depended heavily on putting-out traders (see Table 6-4).

One can see clearly from the above table that the ratio of weaving wages was high in low-income weaving households. The net income of weaving and selling by households only accounted for 8.16% of the total income of households with an income below 50 yuan. The wages paid by putting-out traders accounted for 68.43% of the total income. As the general income increased, the ratio of weaving wages decreased gradually and weaving and selling by households increased. In a household having an annual income between 500 to 600 yuan, the ratio of wages accounted for 6.29% and that of weaving and selling by households increased to 78.52%. Interestingly, in a household with an annual income above 600 yuan, the ratio of wages

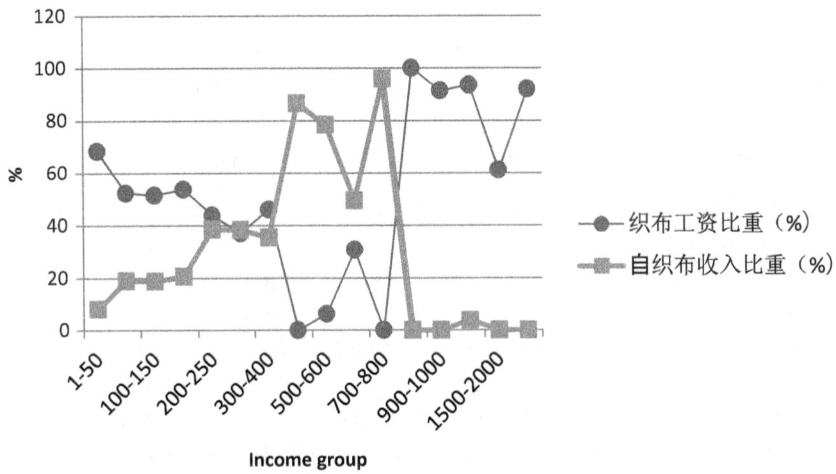

Figure 6-1 Percentage of Income That Is Wage and Percentage of Income That Is Gains Selling Own Products for Weaving Households by Income Groups

(The light line represents the percentage of income that is wage, and the bold line means the percentage of income that is gains selling own products.)

increased suddenly while that of weaving and selling by households reduced rapidly, almost to zero. These two columns of Table 6-4 are depicted as a picture (see Figure 6-1). One can see that the shape of the percentage of weaving wages is represented as the alphabet "u", while that of weaving and selling by households is the alphabet "n".

The picture is very clear. In households with income below 250 yuan, the percentage of wages was obviously higher than that of weaving and selling by households. In households with income between 250 to 400 yuan, the percentage of the two were almost the same. Those households with income between 400 to 800 yuan mostly would not weave for putting-out traders and their earnings mostly came from weaving and selling on their own. However, the earnings of households with income of 800 yuan mostly came from wages. Figure 6-1 clearly shows the following.

Low-income weaving households mainly depended on weaving for putting-out traders because they lacked enough capital and had no economic capacity to shoulder market risks; weaving households with more income mainly depended on weaving and selling on their own, which could bring in much more than if they relied on wages only. The weaving households earning the most also chose putting-out traders, which needs explanation. Let us look at Table 6-4, which comprises data from six big weaving households that each owned three to nine looms and employed six to 14 weavers. They were almost equal to a family factory on a small scale. I will explain later why these factories also relied on putting-out traders.

The Putting-out System and Market Competition

So far, there is a basic understanding of the relationship among the emerging putting-out system, the promotion of the iron-wheel machine and the expansion of the production scale. This was analyzed from production organization. The promotion of production technology and expansion of production scale were based on an expanded market. If there was no expanded market, there would be no impetus for putting-out traders and weaving households to enlarge their production scale. Thus, what was the relationship between the putting-out system and market expansion? We will analyze the different systems of production organization and their competences.

The rivals of the putting-out system in the 1920s and 1930s in China were mainly the following three. The first one was the family homespun industry without the putting-out system. They weaved mainly for their own use, but would sell extra homespun. In some areas with a developed homespun industry, for example, Dingxian County, Hebei Province, weaving households there sold their extra homespun to the northwest through businessmen. The second one was the homespun industry organized as small handicraft factories, which were not frequently seen and mainly distributed in Suzhou, Changzhou, northeast of China and areas outside of the Great Wall. The third and most powerful was the domestic machine weaving industry. The quantity of imported machine-made cloth reduced so rapidly in the 20th century that one needs not pay attention to it.

The putting-out system had three advantages to defeat the aforementioned opponents. I will analyze them one by one.

Quality Control

Some scholars emphasize that one important reason for the long popularity of homespun was its "endurance", which was especially important for common people. Clothing made of homespun could be worn in winter, spring, and summer in proper thickness. After several rounds of mending, it could still be used as the soles of shoes. As the saying goes "you can use a homespun clothing after many times of sewing and mending." This indicates that the quality of homespun was the foundation for its survival. The quality of the homespun in these big weaving areas played an important part in defeating others and selling all over the country. One also notices that the name of homespun varied not only because of its kind but also its producing place. For example, some famous homespun were as follows: Dingbu (cloth) (of Dingxian County) in times using handicraft yarn, Tongbu (cloth) (Nantong) in times using muslin, and homespun from Gaoyang and Weixian Counties. Quality and brand played the most important part when homespun developed a new market.

Compared with machine-made cloth, one could not tell whether homespun was of high quality. Only after the consumer bought it and washed it for the first time, could he know its quality, which was the standard "Experience Goods"[109] in property right economics. If the weaving household smeared lime powder in warp sizing before weaving, he could weave bright, neat white cloth. What is more, one gram of lime powder smeared was equal to one gram of yarn (Hebei Construction, 1928). The specific method was as follows: after weaving the cloth, water it, and then put powder on the surface. Fold it up after drying, then a well made homespun appears (Su, 1984). One can make it heavier by adding more warps and watering (Wu, 1936: 259–261). Fraud was easy, and it was very difficult to check the quality of homespun. Specialists with experience were needed. In all homespun stores in Shanghai, the one who was superior to the boss and mainly in charge of checking quality, was called "Taitou", or the man collecting homespun or checking homespun. They were experts and needed all the time (Xu, 1992: 345). A typical example was as follows:

> "in 1908, located at Sanlintang, Pudong, Tangyixing (the name of homespun store) sold homespun to Niuzhuang (a village), Shandong province etc. in a large scale. The proprietor Tang Yunzhai went to Sunxiaoqiao, Yujieqiao to collect homespun by himself when "Taitou" was ill. Because he had few experiences, and couldn't judge the quality of the homespun well. After selling, he was to be blamed. After that, his business went bankrupt." (Xu, 1992: 366)

One can see that checking the quality was very difficult from the above story. It was easier for many single weaving households or peddlers who weaved and sold homespun to commit fraud under the cash exchange system. The trade of homespun was similar to the "Lemon Model" put

[109] According to Nelson (1970), commodity was divided into two types based on the inner measurement cost. One was "search goods", and the other was "experience goods". The former refers to the commodity which can be measured as high-quality commodity or low-quality commodity before trade. The latter refers to the commodity which can be judged only after using and consuming.

forward by George Akerlof. As information was not symmetrical, shoddy goods filled the market, and the weaving households with high-quality products could not take part in the trade (Akerlof, 1970).

Because of this, famous homespun centers developed corresponding market systems to reduce measuring cost in trade. According to the available historical materials, there were two main market systems, which was called *paizi* (a brand) in Shanghai[110] and the putting-out system in other areas.

From the perspective of property right economics, the development of the putting-out system internalized the relationship between weavers and thread businessmen as authentic relations and finally arrived at the so-called vertical integration, which meant the trade relationship between the weaver and the thread businessman was not equal anymore. The former became the employee of the latter or a part of his institution. According to Thrainn Eggertsson, vertical integration was a market system that solved the "Lemon" problem (Market Practice) (Eggertsson, 1990: 200).

Vertical integration tried to make the trader under its control to prevent the businessman from taking advantage of him (Willamson, 1983). The putting-out trader "is very cautious when employing weaver. They only employ the honest ones with bondsman" (Wu, 936: 28). They also had special notebooks to note down the account of collecting homespun, taking away warp, the general "settled account" and to record the personal and production conditions of their weavers (Wu, 1936: 84–88). After a long time, putting-out traders were familiar with the technology and ethics of their weavers, just like the rating of integrity of a director to his subordinate in a factory. Once the relationship formed, it would be stable because it could reduce the trading cost effectively in the market. Even when homespun industry declined, the putting-out trader "will not separate from his weaver at once because they are close, or the weaver has long establishments in this trade or the weaver makes fine homespun" (Fang and Bi, 1936: 318–322).

[110]Although Shanghai was one of the largest homespun centers of east China, it was still hard to develop the homespun industry in Shanghai, because "brand" played a decisive role. In fact, it was similar to one of the market systems emphasized by Bazel (1980) on the development of high measurement cost. The merchants of Shanghai largely invested in building brand. Some new homespun shops even rented the old brand when it opened up, because the brand meant high market price. Some measures were taken by homespun guilds to punish counterfeit behavior (Xu, 1992: 359–369). Moreover, why the putting-out system did not exist in Shanghai, will be discuss in another book.

As most *Buxian Zhuang* (store selling thread and cloth) or putting-out traders employed between 100 to 300 pieces of looms,[111] a "leader" among several businessmen and weavers was needed, who was generally the richest weaver in a town or village with lots of experience. They shouldered some responsibilities such as introducing new weavers, and urging the weavers to hand in homespun in time. When he encountered people who did not hand in homespun, he would help the businessman to demand raw materials or indemnity. These "leaders" were usually men who enjoyed high prestige, which helped to ensure the credit of weavers (Wu, 1936: 22).

From the perspective of weavers, there were more disadvantages if they were found to be fraudulent. The punishment of deducting pay was light, and they might even be fired by the putting-out trader, which was called "taking machine away" (Zhu, 1935: 573). As I said before, the weaver was mostly a medium or small one who relied heavily on the putting-out trader to solve problems of money and raw materials and shoulder risks. Once the machine was taken away, they could not bear the loss.

From the analysis mentioned earlier, one knows that the reason why homespun in areas adopting the putting-out system could defeat the homespun industry in other areas lay in the strict quality control. But as is known, the biggest enemy of homespun was factory-made cloth. Compared with factory-made cloth, the quality control of the putting-out system was its weakness. Many articles on comparison of economic systems show that the greatest advantage of the factory system replacing the putting-out system lies in its quality control in the Industrial Revolution.[112] The factory system concentrated on production in space, which reduced the supervision cost effectively. No matter how the putting-out system tried to avoid cheating on labor and material, or dishonest deeds, it was hard to avoid these. Compared with the handicraft factory or machine factories, the putting-out system had other advantages besides trying to control quality.

Flexible Scale of Production

In the Republic of China, handicraft weaving mills were not flourishing, and were actually not as common as the putting-out system, which was an important characteristic of rural handicraft industry in China. Amid

[111] In 1923, every merchant rented 170 machines in Baodi (Fang and Bi, 1936: 273), and 200 machines in Gaoyang (Li, 1934).

[112] The discussion of factory system and the putting-out system is in the introduction. We will not explore it here.

Table 6-5 Comparison between Sources of Income of Weaving Households in Different Income Groups

Income Group	Number of Households	Number of Looms	Number of Employees	Loom: Employees	Income of Weaving on the Same Loom① (%)	Income of Selling Homespun② (%)
1–400	320	1.68	0.73	1: 0.43	55.92	18.25
400–800	18	3.06	2.38	1: 0.77	12.33	72.08
800–2500	6	5.83	6.5	1: 1.11	88.62	1.28

①② The so called *Zhi Ding Ji* (weaving on the same loom) and *Zhimaibu* (selling homespun) refer to weaving in *Buxian Zhuang* (weaving house) for putting-out traders and weaving and selling homespun by households, respectively. Both are dialects of Gaoyang County at that time.

Sources: Wu (1936).

the cloth industry in North China, one can hardly see a decent handicraft factory with a certain scale. In the Jiangnan region, although there were relatively many handicraft weaving factories, it had a scale far smaller than that of cloth and thread stores (putting-out merchants) in Jiangyin and Nantong. In Gaoyang, scores of weaving mills appeared due to the rise of weaving jacquard at the end of the 1920s, with the number of looms ranging from 10 to 40. But they were all flashes in the pan, disappearing completely in the 1930s. The surviving family factories, as learnt from the first section, were all hired by the cloth and thread stores instead of competing with them. We have simplified Table 6-4 and divided the weaving households in Gaoyang into three types (see Table 6-5).

The table shows clearly that weaving households with an annual income of 800–2500 yuan had about six looms and 6.5 weavers on average, which could be considered as a standard small family factory. But among the income, 88.62% was paid by putting-out merchants for weaving cloth for them and only 1.28% was earned by weaving cloth. Compared with small weaving households with an annual income lower than 400 yuan, they had a heavier dependence on the putting-out merchant. Why?

Compared with the handicraft factory, the biggest advantage the cloth and thread stores had was that they could rapidly expand the scale of production without large investment and shrink the scale rapidly without high cost when cloth price and demand decreased. So they were the fittest survivors in a market with tough competition and fluctuating price. Generally, they kept a good partnership with skilled and reputed weaving households, even when they shrank the scale of production, for once the

Table 6-6 The Number of Branches of *Buxian Zhuang* (Weaving House) in Gaoyang Village, Xinqiao Town of Gaoyang City

	Period	Number of Branches	Number of Scattered Looms
1	1911–1915	5	750
2	1916–1919	16	2,400
3	1920–1924	6	900
4	1925–1928	12	1,800
5	1932–1933	7	280

Sources: Li (1934); Wu (1936).

market expanded, they could rapidly find producers.[113] In Gaoyang, most of the cloth and thread stores usually hired less than 100 looms. But in the case that the scale needed expanding, they would set up branches in the market towns around Gaoyang City. Like the headquarters, these branches were also capable of putting-out looms. They were very important in expanding scale, for what they needed to do was rent a store front in the center of towns and send someone to display the yarns to sell. It would not cost too much, and the headquarters would take charge of contacting outside markets and managing finance. Besides, the scale of production could be enlarged exponentially. Table 6-6 lists the change of number of branches set up by putting-out merchants of Gaoyang in Shenqiao town over the years, reflecting the flexibility of the putting-out system.

This was the only information concerning the branches of a market town in the Gaoyang cloth region. In this region, there were another two large market towns — Qingta town and Dazhuang town — which were not listed in the table due to lack of materials. But it is most likely they encountered the same situation as Xinqiao town. What impressed us most is that there was a huge difference in the number of branches set up by the putting-out merchants in different periods. When there was an industry downturn, the number of branches was about five, while the number was more than 10 during its two peaks, with some stores opened by the middlemen who were closely linked to the putting-out merchants of Gaoyang not included. These stores were not affiliated to the cloth and

[113]There is no evidence that merchants tended to reduce the workload of weaving households during the economic recession. They recollected the work of part of households, and the rest of the households kept on working. In terms of transaction cost, the latter was wiser though the former may effectively maintain the relationship with households and get certain welfare effects.

thread stores and seldom contacted the markets outside the cloth region. So their only difference from the branches of cloth and thread stores was in the investors, with no difference in operation and management. These middlemen also put out looms and the number put out was usually about 100. Although they were not hired by the putting-out merchants, they delivered and sold the cloth collected to the cloth and thread stores in Gaoyang and were obedient to the will of the latter, making them resemble branches of the putting-out merchants (Li, 1936; Wu, 1936). During 1916–1919, besides the 16 branches which belonged to the Gaoyang cloth and thread stores, there were still dozens of stores set up by the middlemen in Xinqiao town. Thus, we can see the scale of the putting-out system. To describe it visually, the cloth and thread stores and branches controlled by putting-out merchants were like huge octopuses spatially. As long as there were opportunities in the market, they would stretch out their tentacles in all directions while in other periods they would huddle up to save cost.

A characteristic of the putting-out system was that it could change the scale of production in a flexible way with only a low cost, which made small weaving factories an unlikely match. To factories, the best status was maintaining a certain scale and producing constantly. Fixed asset investments such as plants and machines could be exploited to the greatest effect. To the small family factories, they had to reduce the influence imposed by price fluctuations on production while maintaining continuous production. The best way to do this was to be hired by putting-out merchants. On this point, Wu has discussed in detail in his books concerning the homespun cloth industry in Gaoyang.

> "(For small cloth-weaving factories), although weaving and selling on their own (self-employment) could make more money, they often had the following difficulties: (1) their products could not meet the needs of market and were not in demand. If the cloth and thread stores (putting-out merchants) were in urgent need of some products, they would buy it at high price. Some weaving households accordingly weaved this product. But from purchasing raw material to finishing the product, the time spent ranged from ten days to more than half a month. In this period, due to sufficient stock or market change, demand decreased and supply exceeded demand so that it was hard to sell. At this point, the cloth merchants would buy them with a lower price. Because of insufficient capital, the weaving households were unable to maintain their status for a long period. So they were forced to sell the cloth at a low price... (2) Unpredictable change in the supply of raw material and market made the weaving households opt to suffer loss... the price of cotton yarn changed very rapidly with quotations differing every day. If the price difference between two

> packs was ten yuan, the cloth price would undergo great fluctuation. From purchasing raw materials to selling cloth, as least ten days were needed, during which dramatic changes in yarn price often took place. So the profit from weaving cloth was hard to estimate." (Wu, 1936: 96)

In such a case, the best choice for family factories was to contract with putting-out merchants. In the contract, according to the merchants' requirements on the product like size, weight and color, items such as price, delivery date, and quantity should be stipulated in advance and both parties should then honor the contract no matter how the yarn price changed. This kind of contract, in fact, established the employment relationship between putting-out merchants and family factories. To the latter, it could reduce market risk while the former also benefitted from it to some extent. On the one hand, they could have cloth with uniform stipulation; on the other hand, the supply of cloth was secured if the factories honored the contract. This was the root cause of family factories carrying out *Zhi Ding Ji* (putting out looms according to demand).

Small Scale of Capital and Low Debt Asset Ratio

In the eyes of urban machine weaving factories, the two aforementioned advantages were not a big deal. It was because no matter how they controlled the quality, besides thickness and durability, the cloth produced by putting-out merchants was not a match for the uniformity in stipulation and evenness in color of cloth woven by machines. Although putting-out merchants successfully adapted to the changeable yarn market through flexible scale of production, the machine factories were capable of reducing production cost by high productivity (the efficiency of an electronic loom was three times higher than that of the iron-wheel machine) to alleviate the negative impact from market fluctuation. The critical reason why the homespun cloth by putting-out merchants were able to compete with the machine-made cloth was that the former was highly fit for the capital market and industry structure then. This was another advantage enjoyed by putting-out merchants.

In the decade during the early Republic of China when homespun cloth and yarn factories were emerging domestically, the volume of industrial products input from foreign countries declined sharply as the Western powers were preoccupied by the First World War, which created opportunity for domestic industrial development. This period is known by some scholars as "the golden age of Chinese bourgeoisie" (Bergère, 1990). But the industrial development in this period was confined by two factors: industrial structure with a serious imbalance between light industry and heavy industry and the underdeveloped capital market.

Most of the national industries in the early Republic of China were light industries with a predominance for yarn, flour and oil manufacture. Heavy industries, especially the machine-building industry, was very rare. In such a case, the majority of fixed asset investments needed by light industry, especially machinery equipment, were imported from Western countries. Then there came the First World War, which led to less quantity, high price and unfavorable sea transportation for the machines produced by Western countries. In 1913, the freight rate of transportation by water between Shanghai and London was about two pounds and by the summer of 1918, it increased to 50 pounds; in the same period, the freight rate between Shanghai and San Francisco shot up to 60 to 70 dollars from five dollars. Although freight rate decreased rapidly after the war, the strong domestic demand on machinery equipment made the national industry spend heavily on buying machines. But at that time, the fundamental problem lay in the incompleteness of the capital market. Insufficient capital could be seen from very high loan interest rates in banks and money shops (old-style Chinese private banks).[114] Besides speculative activities, the domestic banks seldom loaned on credit, with loan interest rates remaining about 10% (Yan, 1955). In the domestic national industry, capital investment mainly relied on the local money shops in Shanghai. Yet the scale of these money shops were small, and their capital mainly came from deposit money. Hence the leading rate was inevitably very high. Prior to the Revolution of 1911, the money shops in Shanghai offered loans with an annual interest rate of about 7.2% to 12%, sometimes even as high as about 20%. Outside Shanghai, the interest rate of most places was higher. In the same period, the interest rate of Western countries were no more than 5% (Yan, 1955). In such cases, entrepreneurs had to bear very high lending rates besides spending heavily on buying machinery equipment if they intended to open weaving factories. In fact, the imbalance between light industry and heavy industry in the Republic of China was fundamentally caused by lack of resources, because opening cotton mills needed less capital and its scale was more flexible compared with heavy industry (Chen, 1995). The high interest rate caused by lack of resources had always been a

[114]Traditional financial organizations were mainly set up by the merchants of Shanghai, and were popular from the Qing Dynasty and prosperous in the Republic of China.

heavy burden to national industry, which directly affected its profits and competitiveness.

In contrast, the putting-out merchants of homespun cloth had almost been spared such concerns. The sum of average initial capital of the 46 cloth and thread stores in Gaoyang was only 10,800 yuan, of which three stores spent only 1,000 yuan. Those putting-out merchants almost spared no burden brought about by capital investment. In contrast with machine weaving factories with a general investment of ten thousand or several million yuan, the putting-out merchants were "out of debt, out of burden". Table 6-7 compares the data obtained from the cloth and thread stores in Gaoyang and the cotton mills throughout the country respectively, and clearly shows which was better.

The table shows that to produce a bolt of white cloth of similar weight and price, the profit obtained by putting-out merchants was higher than that of machine factory owners whether in the form of absolute value or their ratio to added value. The former's net profit exceeded one-fifth of the

Table 6-7 Comparisons of Cost and Profit between Homespun Industry in Gaoyang and Weaving Factories in Other Areas (1932)

	Gaoyang *Buxian Zhuang*		Weaving Factories across China	
	Eight *Jin* and a Half White Cloth		12 Pounds Fine Cloth in Its True Color	
	Yuan	%	Yuan	%
Cost of yarn	7.08		6.21	
Added value	2.42	100	3.168	100
Wages of production workers	0.8①	33.1	0.587	18.5
Management cost and other expenditures	0.61	25.21	1.324	41.8
Transportation cost	0.52	21.5	0	0
Interests of loan	0	0	0.637	20.1
Tallage	0	0	0.36	11.4
Net profits	0.49	20.3	0.26	8.2
Selling price	9.5	100	9.378	100

① In the table, the weaver's wage under the putting-out system was higher than that of factory workers because here the production cost of every bolt of cloth is calculated. The efficiency of machine-made cloth was three times higher than that of hand-weaving on the same production scale. As a result, the latter's wage was definitely higher than that of the former every year.

Sources: Statistics about Gaoyang County is provided by Wu (1936), while that of weaving factory by Wang and Wang (1935).

added value while the latter's net profit was less than one-tenth. The key lay in the lending rate. As a matter of fact, the latter's direct production cost (wage + management expenditure + freight fare) only took up 60% of added value while the former took up 80%. Hence cloth produced by machine was superior to homespun cloth if judged purely from the perspective of productivity. But the latter had to bear heavy loans because of the high lending rate, taking up 20% of the added value. Without this burden, the latter's net profit would increase to more than three times. Many individual case studies concerning economic history show that large sums of loans were often the main cause leading to losses for Chinese merchants (Tang and Qian, 1997). In fact, by the 1930s, the cotton mills and flour mills opened by Chinese merchants suffered from insolvency and were taken over by financial capital, which resulted from unbearable lending rates instead of war.

However, that the latter's profit rate of each bolt of cloth was lower than the former did not mean that the latter would lose in their competition. As one knows, the efficiency of weaving by machine was four times that of the iron-wheel machine. If both of them had a similar scale, and each produced 12-pound percale and 4.25-kilogram white cloth respectively (see Table 6-7), although the latter's net profit per bolt was half of the former's, its annual gross profit was twice as high as the latter's. But this was obtained under the condition of similar scale. I have detailed in the previous chapter that one of the largest advantages of putting-out merchants was flexibility in scale of production. That is to say, it would expand rapidly when profit rate was high and shrink when profit was low. One is unable to estimate to what extent the characteristic will affect the annual gross profit. It was undoubtedly favorable for merchants in market competition. Therefore, although machine weaving factories were better than the putting-out system in regard to efficiency, they broke even for the advantage of efficiency was offset by the latter's absence of high lending rate and flexible scale of production.

To sum up, one can see that besides the peculiarity in its own organizational form, the reason why the putting-out system enjoyed extreme boom in the handicraft textile industry, became the most important production and market organization in the industry and stood the fight with the machine weaving industry was that it highly catered to the capital and product market environment then. This book never expected that the putting-out system would win the war against the factory system at the expense of reality. It merely tries to explain why this seemingly vernacular organization was able to develop and grow in the industrial age and promote industrialization in some rural areas.

In the last section of this chapter, I will try to present the role this system played in increasing income for peasants, especially in increasing income for small-scale peasant economy which struggled in the trap of involution, to prove the point of view I proposed in the first and second chapters, namely rural industrialization in the Republic of China was able to help the rural economy get rid of involution, instead of waiting until the emergence of town and township enterprises of the 1980s.

Homespun Cloth Industry and Rural Income

Many scholars from the mainland regarded the putting-out system as a system which exploited weaving households by getting commercial capital and usury capital involved into production, and accordingly they adopted a negative attitude toward it (Peng, 1962c; Xu, 1992). Zhao Gang praises the positive influence it brought out on expanding commodity production, but does not analyze in detail the influence it brought out on income distribution of weaving households (Zhao, 1983: 229). In fact, one can gain a rough idea about the influence imposed by the putting-out system on rural income in the analysis of the previous section.

In the rural economy remaining at subsistence level, the largest problem for peasant households to carry out commercial production came from capital and raw material. Fortunately, the putting-out system helped the yeomen who lacked capital with weaving production and also reduced market risk to some extent. So the emergence and development of the putting-out system was closely linked to the weaving production and income increase of medium and small landholding yeomen or even sharecroppers. In Gaoyang, while the absolute number of looms increased, the ratio of looms, which number was determined by the amount of products, to the total also increased rapidly, eventually reaching 80% (Wu, 1936). By 1923, the number of looms which number was determined by the amount of products also took up 72% of the total number (Fang and Bi, 1936).

Most of those who weaved cloth according to demand were medium and small landholding yeomen or sharecroppers who could not afford to buy looms or raw materials. They increased income through being hired by putting-out merchants and obtaining wages.

> "... And the twelfth year of the Republic (1923) — during the year , the wages employers pay also reach a huge amount of 1,253,000 yuan, which is to the 80% of the yearly income of the tenant and Chief weavers. Such employment

weavers are mostly made up of Sharecroppers, whose weaving income four times its farm income..." (Fang and Bi, 1936: 282)

According to the calculation of Fang Xianting and Bi Xianghui, in 1923, the average net income[115] of weaving households who weaved cloth according to demand was 105 yuan, equivalent to four times of the average farm income. In Gaoyang, according to the survey of 382 households in the weaving district by Wu, the average net income of 344 weaving households was 120.71 yuan, while their average farm net income was 27.96 yuan. The former was 4.3 times that of the latter (Wu, 1936: 142).

Although the wage of weaving households was a piece-rate wage, the risk of exposure to market price fluctuations was smaller than weaving sellers. In other words, the putting-out system made the wage income of the woven households relatively stable. This argument has already been briefly mentioned, but most scholars of this field are opposed to this view. An important discovery in *China Cotton Textile Manuscripts* by Yan Zhongping is that, operating with the same number of cloth, buyers invested 26% more of capital than the general dealer. The following is his explanation: "As long as putting-out buyers keep low wages and maintain the difference (between the wages paid by these buyers and the price paid by the general dealers) at a considerable height, their margins are more than general dealers" (Yan, 1955: 291); "If we take the cost of raw materials out of consideration, the direct labor costs account for 34.3% in machine cloth costs, and 56.73% for handicraft cloth.... For putting-out merchants, the most effective method to improve profit is to reduce that 56.73% labor costs" (Yan, 1937: 1039). Is this true? Table 6-8 explains.

This table is a bit complicated, but if the changes of labor time prices, wages and profits in each quarter are plotted as displayed in Figure 6-2, it is more obvious.

First, one can see that the magnitude of change of wages is much smaller than profit by comparing the changes, which can also be seen in the variation of the index on the table. Second, the magnitude of the change of profit runs almost entirely consistent with the change of the actual price of labor. In other words, the benefits and risks of price fluctuations are almost entirely mitigated by the profit changes to maintain a relatively stable wage. This discovery clearly shows that it is unfounded to accuse putting-out merchants of pressuring down wages and shifting market risks.

[115]Net income refers to the income deducting depreciation expense of machine, wage of labor and other expenses of slashing.

Table 6-8 Changes of Wages and Profits in Homespun Industry in Baodi (1922–1929)

Year	*Biao*①	The Real Cost of Labor②	Indicators	Wages	Indicators	Profits	Indicators	Profit Margin
1922	4	0.517	100	0.289	100	0.228	100	12.0
1923	1	0.389	75	0.312	108	0.077	34	3.7
	2	0.463	90	0.357	124	0.106	46	4.9
	3	0.489	95	0.359	124	0.130	57	6.0
	4	0.389	75	0.325	112	0.064	28	2.7
The whole year of 1923		0.412	80	0.335	116	0.077	34	3.4
1926	1	0.401	78	0.244	84	0.157	69	7.8
	2	0.480	93	0.304	105	0.176	77	8.8
	3	0.423	2	0.327	113	0.096	42	5.0
	4	0.607	117	0.333	115	0.274	120	14.5
The whole year of 1926		0.546	106	0.318	110	0.228	100	11.9
1929	1	0.303	59	0.239	83	0.064	28	2.8
	2	0.237	46	0.212	73	0.025	11	1.2
	3	0.222	43	0.156	54	0.066	29	3.1
	4	0.195	38	0.132	46	0.063	28	3.1
The whole year of 1929		0.232	45	0.158	55	0.074	23	3.5

① A period of *Biao* refers to every three months.

② "The real cost of labor" in the table, which is made up of wage and profit, refers to market price deducting the cost of tools and raw materials. In fact, it is the additional value of a product.

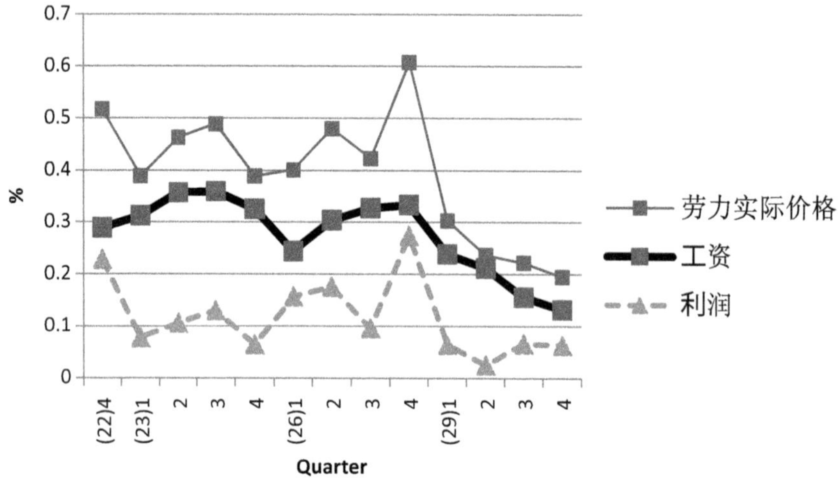

Figure 6-2 Changes of Wages and Profits in Baodi Homespun Industry
(Bold line stands for wages, light line represents profits from the putting-out system, and dotted line is the added value of products.)

In contrast, they protected weaving families from the risks caused by price fluctuations. Material from Baodi can also prove this point, showing similar idea with Figure 6-2:

> "In the merchant employer era, the status of casual workers (wages weaving households) is quite solid. When the hand-woven industry declines, these casual workers are initially complacent, because cloth prices drop does no harm to them as the employer burden all the loss, and they are unlike the master craftsman weavers, who have to burden their own business and be uneasy to the market price fluctuation. That is the reason why weaving households are willingly to work for the merchant." (Fang and Bi, 1936: 318)

While our analysis does not negate buyers' exploitation on weaving households, the profit of weaving sellers was much higher than wages of weaving households.

From the wage comparison between weaving households working for the putting-out merchants and those selling on their own in Baodi, 1923, the income of each bolt of cloth of the latter was 18% higher than that of the former (Fang and Bi, 1936: 300–301).

In Gaoyang, around 1926, the flourishing era of rayon fabric (commonly known as burlap), weaving a bolt of *Minghuage* (the name of a kind of burlap), those working for the putting-out merchants could earn four or

Table 6-9 Information on 382 Weaving Households in Gaoyang①

Nature of Weaving Household	Number of Households	The Percentage of Total Households (%)
Buying materials by households	124	32.5
Weaving by receiving materials from putting-out traders	223	58.3
Buying materials by themselves combined with weaving by receiving materials from putting-out traders	35	9.2
Type of Looms	**Number of Households**	**Average Looms in Every Household (Pieces)**
Using jacquard	107	3
Using plane machine	275	1.5

① Jacquard and plane machines both belonged to the category of iron-wheel machines. A plane machine was used to weave common complanate cotton. A jacquard machine consisted of a "jacquard basket" on the top of a plane machine and could be used to weave a verity of colorful man-made silk (flax). According to Wu, the popularity of jacquard and flax was the main reason why Gaoyang weaving area thrived in the 1920s (Wu, 1936: 24–27).

Sources: Wu (1936).

five yuan and those selling on their own could earn five or six yuan (Wu, 1936: 27). It seems there was little difference, but it was not the case.

A further analysis is made based on the survey data collected by Wu of 382 weaving families in Gaoyang. Table 6-9 is based on the data listed in the book.

According to what Wu describes in another paper, weaving households working for putting-out merchants accounted for 85% of people who weaved plane cloth, while weavers selling cloth on their own took up more than 60% of those who used jacquard machines. One can infer that 107 weaving households with jacquard machines were mostly weave sellers (124 in total); and 275 households weaving plane cloth were mainly given by the weaving machine and fixed machine sellers and both (258 in total). As can be seen, weaving households selling cloth on their own took up a small proportion (roughly one-third), but they had expensive jacquard machines with high output value, and the average household loom weaving output was also twice the given machine family. In other words, woven sellers owned much more capital than weaving households. Accordingly, the production capacity and output value of the former were higher than those of the latter. The data of Wu show that the households weaving only cotton cloth (woven scheduled, plane machine) weaved the least number of cloth per household on average throughout the year in all kinds of weaving households, approximately 140 bolts; while those who weaved both cotton and linen weaved the maximum number of cloth per household on average, 120.67 bolts of cotton cloth and 396.67 bolts of linen every year. Per cloth, the income difference between woven given machine and weaving sellers was not great, but taking into account its own differences on the assets, labor and production capacity, annual income differences were necessarily larger than imagined. According to the annual output of the above,[116] the difference between the most production and the least production of the two types was up to more than four times (Wu, 1938: 683).

Weaving sellers had strong capital ability to solve businessmen's restrictions on buying yarn. They also tried to eliminate restrictions on labor to expand production scale. As said earlier in this chapter, this kind of family was generally large in scale — the number of young and old, women and children was big — which was quite appropriate for weaving:

> "The first is the workers of the family master craftsman system. The master of the house is probably the weaver and chief overseer, and presides over all business on the operation, such as the obtain of raw materials, sales of product, the settlement of the wages and so on. While the light work, such as *Jiang jing*, *Luo jing*, *Zheng jing*, *Zhuang zhi* and *Luo wei*, is almost done by the families." (Wu, 1938: 683)

If there were insufficient family members, the woven sellers' families would hire workers. In fact, the data of Gaoyang show that among 382 families, there were 154 families with workers or apprentices, and the number of artificial jacquard cloth was the largest. The number of hires of woven sellers' families could indirectly show and explain why the number of woven sellers' looms were large and the output value was high.

So far, we have analyzed the relationship between the system and income distribution in the weaving center, and one can see that the prevalence of the putting-out system was the most important factor to affect the farmers' income distribution in several big weaving areas of the North China Plain. Most self-selling weavers boasted large capital and labor, and they accounted for almost all cash transaction systems of

[116] The data on local raw material and cloth price are deficient; we have to calculate according to wage. At that time, weaving households tended to hire laborers to weave; the wage of laborers weaving flat cloth was 50 yuan, laborer of jacquard 60 yuan, with an income difference of between 15% to 20%, and so the profit of a gunny amounted to 1.15 to 12 bolts of flat income.

production and the market. Their profits were the return of market on capital and entrepreneurs' quality. However, due to the putting-out system, small farmers and even tenants who had been unable to participate in large-scale commercial production came to own machines and weave cloth, and together with the "weaver-sellers" farmers to join the production of homespun. Though their earnings were not as high as the entrepreneurs, their income was generally increased, This can be explained by "in these years, although the floods, droughts have happened frequently, people in the county (Baodi) are still well-off and not slackened" (Hebei Provincial Government Department of Construction, 1928: 61). Unfortunately, one cannot find data about the weaving households' income distribution in the three weaving areas where the putting-out system was prevalent. One gets the above view through analyzing the data from some clips and text. In fact, one can only find comparative systematic data about income distribution of weaving families in areas where the putting-out system was prevalent in the hand-made areas in Nantong, Jiangsu Province. The data are shown in Table 6-10.

The data distribution in the table aligns with our conclusion. The proportion of weaving industry income distribution among farmers was saddle-shaped, namely the lower and higher income farmers were involved in homespun production to a considerable extent. Accounting for the fact that the income share of the weaving industry was higher in the three weaving areas of North China, one can conclude that when the income of wealthy woven households increased, a large number of small- and medium-sized organizations' households were involved in homespun production with increasing income.

In the following, let us take the rise of the Gaoyang weaving area as an example to investigate the dynamic relationship between the system and income.

One knows that the scope of the three weaving areas was not concentrated in the three counties only, but included several counties surrounding the center. Its prosperity, and the degree of expansion were also different. During the most prosperous period of Gaoyang cloth area, it included four to five surrounding areas such as Qingyuan, Renqiu, Lixian, An'xin and even Suning Counties. These weaving areas all experienced an expansion process. To examine this process, Gaoyang shall be taken as an example.

Before the rise of the putting-out system, Gaoyang city and several surrounding towns, such as Dazhuang, Xinqiao and Qingta towns, mostly practiced in the system of yarn for cloth or cash transactions. In fact,

Table 6-10 Status of Average Household Weaving Income in That of Agricultural and Weaving Income in Nantong①

Total Net Income Group (Yuan)	Number of Households	Percentage of Income from Weaving in Total Income %
1–49.9	13	33.5
50–99.9	35	22.5
100–149.9	8	9.6
150–199.9	4	7.7
200–249.9	1	8.3
250–299.9	1	34.7
300–399.9	1	40.7
400–	—	—
Total	63	20.7

① In the original text, there are statistics about Dingxian County. But as one knows, there was no putting-out system in Dingxian County and the situation there was very special, thus we do not use statistics about it here. Peace church vigorously developed rural areas in Dingxian County in the 1920s and 1930s, which changed greatly the economic structure of Dingxian County. Judging from the statistics on monthly newspaper of Hebei Province, the output value in every acre of land per household in Dingxian County reached 42.7 yuan, which was much higher than that of other counties. At that time, more than 90% of the total households in Hebei Province had an output value of lower than 10 yuan every household. The much higher degree of agricultural output value would definitely change the flow of the capital. Thus those rich peasants would invest more on agriculture.

Sources: Yan (1955): 283.

weaving households were considered as weaving sellers. Initially, when the putting-out system rose in Gaoyang city, the *Buxian Zhuang* that controlled the raw materials and cloth excluded the original cloth traders, so the latter transferred to several towns of the neighboring districts. The situation of this time was that most weaving households in Gaoyang became employed weaving households. A large number of small subsistence farmers also joined the weaving ranks. The iron-wheel machine was widely used, and the cloth production largely increased, but the several surrounding towns were relatively slow. Although their hand-woven industry also developed, most of the weaving households sold cloth on their own. Compared with the Gaoyang weaving households, they were more constrained by capital and labor, and poor farmers were not able to be engaged in continuous cloth.

However, the putting-out system soon expanded into several surrounding regions, and then the towns also implemented the system. This process only took three to four years (1912–1916). Compared with 1915, in 1920, the number of scattered machines and *Buxian Zhuang* increased more than twice in Xinqiao town, and once in Qingta town. At the same time, in Gaoyang, there were more and more weaving households selling on their own, while the surrounding towns showed the opposite trend, weaving for putting-out traders mainly (Li, 1934; Wu, 1936). On one hand, as weaving households in Gaoyang city had generally accumulated certain capital by that time, they could conduct independent production and even hire workers. As a result, the income of weaving households working for putting-out merchants declined comparatively. On the other hand, more poor farmers weaved for putting-out traders in the surrounding towns. For farmers, not only the farmers with capital and labor could conduct continued weaving production, but almost all farmers could get profit. For wiring providers, expanding forces to the surrounding towns not only enlarged the scale of production effectively, but also saved a lot of production costs. In 1933, the wage gap between Gaoyang city and Qingta town was already quite large, for the wage of the former was almost twice that of the latter for every 11 *jin* of white cloth (Li, 1934).

It can be seen that the income distribution of the farmers in the towns surrounding Gaoyang was almost entirely dominated by the expansion of the putting-out system. Farmers in Gaoyang went through three stages, from being weaver-seller to working for putting-out merchants, then back to weaver-seller. Poor farmers experienced the process of inability to have financial capacity to weave to weaving for the putting-out traders to accumulate certain strength, and then started to sell cloth on their own. But the towns surrounding Gaoyang experienced a two-stage process of self-sellers and weavers-for-the-trader. With the extension of the putting-out system, more and more farmers weaved for the putting-out trader. To put it in a simple way, before the implementation of the putting-out system, limited by the capital and labor, farmers mainly sold their cloth on their own, and a large number of rich peasants or landlords and small cloth merchants set up cloth stalls as the intermediary for profit. Farmers with capital and labor gained the majority on commodity production. After the implementation of the putting-out system, although weaving households working for putting-out traders obtained lower wages than weavers in Gaoyang and those who sold on their own, every family could weave. Therefore, the profit of the weaving industry was also transferred from the better-off farmers to everyone.

Chapter 7

Conclusion: Commercialization, Institutional Change and Rural Industrialization

In the eyes of economic historians, the Chinese economy in the Ming and Qing Dynasties had two different appearances. On the one hand, studies by some scholars show that under the pressure of population growth, economic growth was maintained at the level of Song Dynasty since the agricultural technology and labor productivity peaked in the Song Dynasty (960–1279), and there was no improvement after that (Perkins, 1969). This was due to the fast growth of population that created negative pressure on the increase of per capita production and technological progress. A large number of surplus labor forces existed in the economic system, and land was delicately divided into many scattered pieces. Peasants adopted intensive cultivation, investing surplus labors into limited farm land, and aimed at the increase of overall production with the decline of labor productivity. This phenomenon was called "High-level Trap" by Mark Elvin, and "involution" by Philip Huang.[117] On the other hand, some other scholars are impressed by the Chinese economy in that historical period. According to Angus Maddison's estimation, China and Europe were the two largest economic systems in the world before the Industrial Revolution. In 1700, the gross domestic

[117] "Involution" by Philip Huang is applied to the late Qing Dynasty and the beginning of the Republic of China. His monographs on the economy of Ming and Qing Dynasties are comparatively fewer. But if we study the content of "involution", we can find that it is similar to the "High-level Trap", just with a different name.

product (GDP) of China and that of Europe accounted for 23.1% and 23.3% respectively of the total GDP of the world, while it came to be 33.4% and 26.6% respectively in 1820, when those ratios of India, Japan, America and Russia respectively were 15.7%, 3.0%, 1.8% and 4.8%. As for the rate of economic growth, China and Europe were the two fastest-growing regions apart from America and Russia. Between 1700 and 1820, China had an annual GDP growth of 0.85% and that of Europe was 0.68%, both of which were higher than that of the world's average (0.57%) (Maddison, 1998). But how did the Chinese economy in the Ming and Qing Dynasties grow? According to some economic historians and the analysis in Chapters 2 and 3 of this book, what sustained the economic growth were the following: the expansion of the domestic market and the prosperity of remote trades, regional specialization and the development in division of labor, which were also the features of the Smithian growth, among which the prosperity of the cotton textile industry in the south of the Yangtze River and the booming national cotton trade thereafter especially stood out (Feuerwerker, 1970, 1995).

Judging from the above, on the one hand, the Chinese economy in the Ming and Qing Dynasties showed clear characteristics of Smithian growth, similar to the condition of Europe before the Industrial Revolution. While on the other hand, it had features of the so called involution resulting from an excess of population and stagnation in labor productivity. What impacts did these have on rural industrialization and its further growth? The logic of "involution" is simple: the surplus labor force consumes a lot of the excess agricultural products, simply leaving no room for the development of the rural industrialization. Even if rural handicraft industry does exist, it is merely involutionized rural industry, which features share with those of agriculture and whose gains are only for earning a living. In other words, "to work or not, a man always makes a living. Not counting the time spent and the food consumed, we will run a surplus naturally." Judging from this, the economy in the Ming and Qing Dynasties ran into the blind-alley-like "trap" or "involution" and could not give birth to real industrialization and "develop".

I have tried to prove in Chapters 3 and 4 that in the Chinese economy before modern times, Smithian growth gradually defeated Involution growth, generating the rural industrialization in some areas like that of Western Europe before the Industrial Revolution, where it was named "proto-industrialization". There was nothing more prominent and typical than the cotton textile industry in Songjiang prefecture in the Ming and

Qing Dynasties. It shared several traits with proto-industrialization in Western Europe:

(1) Producing for remote trade. The Songjiang Cloth was known as "offering the world clothing", and was sold throughout the country at the end of the Ming Dynasty. As to the scale of the market, it was not inferior to that of the British wool textile industry at the same period. According to Chao Gang, the market demand for Songjiang Cloth, between the 16th and 17th century, was as much as the global market exploited by Britain when the Industrial Revolution had just ended (Chao, 1977).

(2) The development of regional specialization. In the Ming and Qing Dynasties, cotton in Songjiang prefecture and silk in Suzhou had been regional specialized products. As one knows, for most of the year, women in Songjiang prefecture had been spinning and weaving; meanwhile, Hunan Province and Hubei Province had already been specialized bases of grain, providing a large amount of them for the Yangtze River delta in the Qing Dynasty (Wu, 1985). This relationship was exactly similar to that between the south and the north in Britain before the Industrial Revolution (Jones, 1974).

(3) The significant increase of peasants' income. To examine the involution of an industry, the key is to observe whether the marginal productivity of labor begins to decline. Chapter 4 has investigated in detail the weaving women's marginal productivity of labor, which indicates that with the enlargement of weaving scale it did not descend, but ascended during the more than 200 years between the end of the Ming Dynasty (1573) and the flourishing age in the Qing Dynasty (1795), increasing from 1.15 litres of rice at the end of the Ming Dynasty to 1.5 litres of rice in the Qing Dynasty, an increase of 30%. Furthermore, women weaving and men plowing made almost equal contributions to the family's net income, which meant that "men plowing the fields and women weaving cloth" made the best of their respective advantages here. While the opportunity cost of both weaving by men and plowing by women was higher, according to Li Bochong, in the south of the Yangtze River, the division of labor between women and men resulted in the maximizing of their economic profits, which cannot be compared to traditional "men plowing the fields and women weaving cloth" (Li, 2000).

The comparison teaches us that population pressure or involution might not always be a trap difficult to escape, and it could also bring proto-industrialization and Smithian growth thereafter. In Songjiang, industrialization made this area the richest in the world from the Ming Dynasty to the Qing Dynasty. One also notices that the Yangtze River Delta centered by Songjiang prefecture had been the most densely populated region in the world and it was in this region that proto-industrialization appeared for the first time in China. As one has seen, the economic growth in this area was typical Smithian growth other than Involution growth, which brought new challenges to the traditional ideas. Will dense population always result in economically involutionary behaviors?

The answer is obviously negative. The market trade plays a key role. What sustained proto-industrialization and economic growth in Songjiang prefecture was a national market created by remote cloth merchants, who "drove on frozen river, sailed in the Yangtze River, ate in the wind and slept in the boats, and then reached Suzhou and Changzhou." Overpopulation was not always bad, and it was the vibrant and competitive market that was the good medicine to cure "involution". The experiences of Songjiang prefecture demonstrated that excess population became a great power for further economic growth with this medicine.

The role played by the market became more prominent at the end of the Qing Dynasty and in the early Republic of China, which, in the eyes of some scholars, was not a wonderful prescription to help the world, but the chief criminal pushing smallholders to the edge of bankruptcy. The process of commercialization and rapid market expansion brought about by the invasion of capitalism, had not made agriculture get rid of the pressure of overpopulation, but entrapped it further into involution. I have made an elaborate discussion about it, so unnecessary details will no longer be offered here. My discussion contradicts with that argument by investigating the destiny of rural cotton textile industry in the process of commercialization. Certainly, the development of handicraft industry in some regions in North China and south of the Yangtze River was far from enough to represent the declining state of overall Chinese rural economy in the commercialization process, nor the true features of the handicraft industry in most regions. But my thesis aims at finding out industries where peculiar changes had taken place in the commercialization process, which precisely makes it clear that villages did not always collapse in the process of commercialization, but rather developed step-by-step.

First, the rapidly declining cotton textile industry in Songjiang prefecture will be examined. On the surface, by World War I, homespun industry in Songjiang prefecture had turned from "clothing the whole world" to "rarely seen" weaving women, which ascribed to the competition from machine-made cloth by most scholars. Compared to homespun, machine-made cloth were known throughout the country for their high quality and low price. It was reasonable that machine-made cloth forced homespun to the edge of total collapse. However, my research demonstrates that the rapid decline did not stem from the competition with machine-made cloth, because even at the eve of the First World War when machine-made cloth was popular, the marginal income of weaving women in Songjiang was one-quarter higher than that in the heyday of the Qing Dynasty (2 litres of rice : 1.5 litres of rice). When faced with such a high marginal income, how can one say that the reason for women to quit weaving was due to the competition with machine-made cloth?

Actually, it was precisely the "decline" that demonstrated the rapid economic development in Songjiang prefecture. Most areas administrated by Songjiang prefecture are now located in Shanghai, and it was just the early Republic of China that saw Shanghai rising as the first major city in China. The development of cities provided many chances of earning far more than the cloth industry in Songjiang for peasants, and rural women would rather go to Shanghai "to be female nurses" than continue to stay in villages weaving. Meanwhile, a large number of rural industries represented by knitting and towel factories emerged in the rural areas in Songjiang, and women could "work in factories", and earn higher pay than cloth weaving. Economic development resulted in the price of labor rising so rapidly in this region that hiring helping hands in busy seasons became a big problem. Both *Changgong* (farm laborer hired by the year) and temporary laborers were supposed to provide "streaky pork" as their food.

Second, the "decline" of the homespun industry in Songjiang prefecture did not mean the decline of the whole homespun industry. As one knows, when peasants in Songjiang gave up weaving and striving for other occupations, the homespun industry in Jiangyin, Changshu, and Nantong, which were far from Shanghai, sprung up quickly and reached prosperity rapidly. Homespun industries in those regions were still organized by cloth businessmen in Shanghai. Although the profits from weaving cloth were little and insignificant for peasants in Songjiang, for those in Jiangyin, Changshu, and Nantong, the interest in weaving cloth was much higher than for farm work. The situation of "choosing to weave and wasting lands" happened in Jiangyin. All of these illustrate that the emergence of some homespun weaving zones did not result from peasants' involution behaviors in the late Qing Dynasty and the early Republic of China, but stemmed from peasants' pursuit of maximum profits from non-agricultural employment.

Last but not least, the prosperity of homespun did not only show in cloth zones in Songjiang geographically moving out, but also in the rapid rising of the three famous cloth zones in North China. These three zones were located respectively in Baodi, Gaoyang in Hebei Province and Weixian in Shandong Province, where the homespun industry was extremely prosperous in the 1930s. Almost every household devoted themselves to weaving cloth, and many households even owned more than two looms and employed others to weave. The earnings of weaving cloth were twice as much as those of agriculture in these weaving zones. Although influenced by the fierce competition with both machine-made cloth and domestic factory cloth, these zones have survived for decades. Specifically, the zone in Weixian was on the rise when Japan's invasion of China started in 1937, and did not show any signs of declining.

The findings above suggest that no matter how "stagnant" and "outdated" the rural economy was in the late Qing Dynasty and the early Republic of China, population pressure combined with commercialization produced another possibility. In brief, this possibility was rural industrialization. The phenomena of rural industrialization reminds us to answer the question proposed at the start of my research, that is, the most important question in Chinese modern economic history: what was the impact of commercialization? In my opinion, commercialization not only drove the development of modern industries in cities, but also started the process of rural industrialization, which was interrupted by massive wars when it had just begun.

I have attempted to answer another question in this research, that is: how did commercialization drive the process of rural industrialization? In the late Qing Dynasty and the early Republic of China, most regions in China, especially the eastern provinces, were all heavily influenced by Western culture and civilization. As one knows, it was the wide use of muslin and spreading of the iron-wheel machine produced by commercialization that brought opportunities for the prosperity of homespun and industrialization. This was an essential condition for the handicraft industry to get out of involution and step into industrialization as mentioned earlier. One can imagine that the handicraft industry remained in the state of self-producing and self-consuming without the impact of commercialization. However, the raw material and change of technology brought by commercialization was a necessary but not sufficient condition for industrialization.

Across the entire eastern provinces, there were no regions free from the influence of commercialization. The muslin was widely used all over the country, but why was industrialization activated only in some regions?

The quantitative analysis done in this book demonstrates that institutional change was the key to industrialization in these regions. Institutional change indicated a huge change in the handicraft industry in organization and forms of production under the influence of an expanding market and input of muslin. Specifically, it was the process through which the putting-out system emerged, developed and replaced the decentralized household management and self-serve mode. Judging by appearances, it did not change a lot from weaving and consuming by households to be employed by putting-out traders, because the decentralized household management remained. In fact, both the forms of production organization and market institution have changed tremendously. In the analysis of the textile industry in more than 400 counties in the five eastern provinces, one can see that the rise of the putting-out system determined the prosperity of homespun industry significantly. While the emerging of the putting-out system depended on some exogenous variables in an area, for example, transportation condition, population density, whether there was a weaving tradition, etc., these exogenous variables did not directly determine whether the cloth industry could develop in certain regions, but worked by having an impact on the emerging of the putting-out system. In Chapter 5, I have proven the mechanism with a two-stage analytical model.

In Chapter 6, I have answered the question why the putting-out system played such a vital role through system analysis. The process of commercialization resulting from the input of foreign capital, created the conditions for the emergence and prosperity of the putting-out system. After its coming into being, the rural handicraft industry organized by the putting-out system had to compete directly against machine-made goods. This process simplified the evaluation of the one-dimensional process of commercialization. At least from the point of view of the homespun industry, it responded positively to the impact of commercialization via institutional change. The institutional change was positive and effective, which not only enabled the homespun industry to compete with muslin, but also drew in competition with domestic factory-made cloth.

According to the traditional comparison theory of economic systems, the putting-out system is inferior to the factory system and is no match for it. The Industrial Revolution was actually the factory system's huge triumph over the putting-out system. My emphasizing on the strong influence of the putting-out system does not aim at overthrowing the system comparison theory and proving its superiority to the factory system, but uncovers the myth of the putting-out system being undefeated in the homespun industry by analysis.

By providing yarn and taking back cloth, supplying looms and collecting cloth, putting-out traders offered poor peasants opportunities to be engaged in weaving, while they also got a large number of cheap labor. Simultaneously, from the perspective of organization of the putting-out system, via the close relationship between putting-out traders and weaving households, the putting-out traders controlled the quality of homespun effectively and made their cloth competitive. As to the market circumstances at that time, the Chinese economy in the late Qing Dynasty and the early Republic of China was an underdeveloped economic system in shortage of capital. Machine-made goods, domestic factory-made goods, products from the handicraft industry and the putting-out system competed with each other fiercely. After my analysis and demonstration, one can see that the putting-out system had some unique advantages in that environment, for example, flexible scale of production, small assets, and low liability ratios, etc. which were suitable for the circumstances of unstable markets and immature capital market compared with machine weaving factory in cities. In this type of market, the putting-out system happened to be present, avoided its shortfalls but unfolded its advantages. This is where the secret of the prosperity of homespun industry really lay.

Bibliography

Articles and Books in English

Akerlof, G. (1970), "The Market for 'Lemons': Quality Uncertainty and the Market Mechanism", *Quarterly Journal of Economics* **84**: 488–500.

Aldirich, R. A. (1987). "Later-Center or Early-starter? New Views on French Economic History", *The Journal of European Economic History* **16**: 89–100.

Barclay G. W., Coale, A. J., Stoto, M. A. and Trussell, T. J. (1976), "A Reassessment of the Demography of Traditional Rural China", *Population Index* **42**(4): 606–635.

Belfanti, C. (1993), "Rural Manufactures and Rural Proto-industries in the 'Italy of the Cities' from the Sixteenth through the Eighteenth Century", *Continuity and Change* **8**: Special Number on Proto-industrialization.

Berg, M. (1985), *The Age of Manufactures, 1700–1820.* London: Routledge.

Bergère, Marie-Claire, *The Golden Age of the Chinese Bourgeoisie, 1911–1937.* Cambridge University Press.

Brandt, L. (1987), "Farm Household Behavior, Factor Markets, and the Distributive Consequences of Commercialization in Early Twentieth-Century China", *Journal of Economic History* **3**: 711–737.

Brandt, L. (1989), *Commercialization and Agricultural Development: Central and Eastern China*, 1870–1937. New York: Cambridge University Press.

Brandt, L. and Sands, B. (1994), "Land Concentration and Income Distribution in Republican China", in T. G. Rawski and M. Li (ed), *Chinese History in Economic Perspectives.* Berkeley: University of California Press.

Braudel, F. (1985), *Civilization and Capitalism, 15th–18th Century.* New York: Harper & Row.

Braun, R. (1966), "The Impact of Cottage Industry on an Agricultural Population", in D. Landes (ed), *The Rise of Capitalism.* New York: McMillan.

Braun, R. (1987), "Early Industrialization and Demographic Changes in the Canton of Zurich", in C. Tilly (ed), *Historical Studies of Changing Fertility.* Princeton: Princeton University Press.

Eggertsson, T. (1990), *Economic Behavior and Institutions.* Cambridge: Cambridge University Press.

Elvin, M. (1973), *The Pattern of the Chinese Past: A Social and Economic Interpretation.* Stanford: Stanford University Press.

Feuerwerker, A. (1970), "Handicraft and Manufactured Cotton Textiles in China, 1871–1910", *Journal of Economic History* **30**: 338–378.

Feuerwerker, A. (1995), *Studies in the Economic History of Late Imperial China: Handicraft, Modern Industry, and the State.* Ann Arbor: The University of Michigan.

Geertz, C. (1963), *Agricultural Involution: The Process of Ecological Change in Indonesia.* Berkeley: University of California Press.

Gullickson, G. (1983), "Agriculture and Cottage Industry: Redefining the Causes of Proto-industrialization", *Journal of Economic History* **43**: 831–850.

Hausman, J. (1978), "Specification Tests in Econometrics", *Econometrica* **46**: 1251–1271.

Huang, P. (1985), *The Peasant Economy and Social Change in North China.* Stanford: Stanford University Press.

Huang, P. (1990), *The Peasant Family and Rural Development in the Yangzei Delta, 1350–1988.* Stanford: Stanford University Press.

Jenkins, D. T. (1975), *The West Riding Wool Textile Industry, 1700–1835.* Edington, Wiltshire: Pasold Research Found Ltd.

Johnson, D. G. (1999), "Population and Economic Growth", *China Economic Review* **10**: 1–16.

Jones, E. (1974), *Agriculture and the Industrial Revolution.* Oxford: Oxford University Press.

Jones, E. L. (1981), "Agriculture, 1700–80", in R. Floud and D. McCloshey (eds), *The Economic History of Britain since 1700.* Cambridge: Cambridge University Press.

Jones, S. R. H. (1982), "The Organization of Work: A Historical Dimension", *Journal of Economic Behavior and Organization* **3**: 117–137.

Jones, S. R. H. (1983), "Technology and the Organization of Work: A Reply", *Journal of Economic Behavior and Organization* **4**: 63–66.

Jones, S. R. H. (1987), "Technology, Transaction Costs and the Transition to Factory Production in the Britain Silk Industry 1700–1870", *The Journal of Economic History* **47**: 71–96.

Kremer, M. (1993), "Population Growth and Technological Change: On Million B. C. to 1990", *Quarterly Journal of Economics* **108**: 681–716.

Kriedte, P. *et al.* (1981), *Industrialization before Industrialization.* Cambridge: Cambridge University Press.

Kung, J. K. and Liu, S. (1997), "'Farmers' Preference Regarding Ownership and Land Tenure in Post-Mao China: Unexpected Evidence from Eight Counties", *The China Journal* **38**: 33–63.

Landes, D. (1986), "What Do Bosses Really Do?", *The Journal of Economic History* **66**: 585–623.

Landes, D. (1997), *The Unbound Prometheus.* Cambridge: Cambridge University Press.

Levine, D. (1977), *Family Formation in an Age of Nascent Capitalism (Studies in Social Discontinuity).* New York: Cambridge University Press.

Lipson, E. (1921), *The History of Woollen and Worested Industries.* London: A. & C. Black Ltd.

Maddison. A. (1998), *Chinese Economic Performance in the Long Run.* Paris: OECD.

Mager, W. (1993), "Proto-industrialization and Proto-industry: The Uses and Drawbacks of the Two Concepts", in S. Ogilvie (ed), *Continuity and Change* **8**: Special Number on Proto-Industrialization.

Magnusson, L. (1991), "From Verlag to Factory: The Contest for Efficient Property Rights", in B. Gustafsson (ed), *Power and Economic Institutions: Reinterpretations in Economic History.* Worcester: Billing & Sons Ltd.

Mann, S. (1992), "Women's Work in the Ningbo Area, 1900–1936", in T. Rowski and L. Li (eds), *Chinese History in Economic Perspective.* Berkeley: University of California Press.

Manning, W. G., Duan, N., and Rogers, W. H. (1987), "Monte Carlo Evidence on the Choice between Sample Selection and Two-Part Models", *Journal of Econometrics* **35**: 59–82.

Mantoux, P. (1983), *The Industrial Revolution in the Eighteenth Century: An Outline of the Beginning of the Modern Factory System in England.* Chicago: University of Chicago Press.

Marglin, S. (1974), "What Do Bosses Do?" *Review of Radical Political Economy* **6**: 60–112.

McCloskey, D. (1994), "The Industrial Revolution 1780–1860: A Survey", in R. Floud and D. N. McCloskey (eds), *The Economic History of Britain since 1700.* Cambridge: Cambridge University Press.

Medick, H. (1981), "The Proto-industrial Family Economy", in P. Kriedt, H. Medick and J. Schlumbohn (eds), *Industrialization before Industrialization.* London: Cambridge University Press.

Mendels, F. (1969), *Industrialization and Population Pressure in Eighteenth Century Flanders.* New York: Wisconsin University Press.

Mendels, F. (1972), "Proto-industrialization: The First Phase of the Industrialization Process", *Journal of Economic History* **32**: 241–261.

Mendels, F. (1973), "Agriculture and Peasant Industry in Eighteenth-century Flanders", in W. Parker and E. Jones (eds), *European Peasants and Their Markets.* Princeton: Princeton University Press.

Mendels, F. (1975), "Agriculture and Peasant Industry in Eighteenth-century Flanders", in W. Parker and E. Jones (eds), *European Peasants and Their Markets.* Princeton: Princeton University Press.

Mendels, F. (1980), "Seasons and Regions in Agriculture and Industry during the Process of Industrialization", in S. Pollard (ed), *Region and Industrialization*: 177–195.

Mokyr, J. (1976), *Industrialization in the Low Countries, 1795–1850.* New Haven: Yale University Press.

Myers, R. (1970), *The Chinese Peasant Economy: Agricultural Development in Hopei and Shantung, 1890–1949.* Cambridge: Harvard University Press.

Nelson, P. (1970), "Information and Consumer Behavior", *Journal of Political Economy*, **78**: 311–329.
North, D. (1981), *Structure and Change in Economic History*. New York: Norton.
North, D. and Thomas, R. (1973), *The Rise of the Western World: A New Economic History*. Cambridge: Cambridge University Press.
Ogilvie, S. (1993), "Proto-industrialization in Europe", *Continuity and Change* **8**: 159–179.
Pomeranz, K. (2000), *The Great Divergence: Europe, China, and the Making of the Modern World Economy*. Princeton: Princeton University Press.
Rawski, T. (1989), *Economic Growth in Prewar China*. Berkeley: University of California Press.
Rule, J. (1981), *The Experience of Labour in Eighteenth-century Industry*. London: St Martin's Press.
Skinner, W. G. (1966), "Marketing and Social Structure in Rural China", *Journal of Asian Studies* **24**: 3–44.
Smith, R. M. (1981), "Fertility, Economy, and Household Formation in English over Three Centuries", *Population and Development Review* **7**: 595–622.
Szostak, R. (1989), "The Organization of Work: The Emergence of the Factory Revisited", *Journal of Economic Behavior and Organization* **11**: 343–358.
Thrisk, J. (1961), "Industries in the Countryside", in F. Fisher (ed), *Essays in the Economic and Social History of Tudor and Stuart England*. Cambridge: Cambridge University Press.
Williamson, O. (1980), "The Organization of Work: A Comparative Institutional Assessment", *Journal of Behavior and Organization* **1**: 5–38.
Williamson, O. (1983), "Credible Commitments: Using Hostages to Support Exchange", *American Economic Review* **73**: 519–540.
Williamson, O. (1985), *The Economic Institutions of Capitalism*. New York: The Free Press.
Wong, R. B. (1997), *China Transformed: Historical Change and the Limits of European Experience*. Ithaca: Cornell University Press.
Yeh, K. C. (1965), *The Economy of the Chinese Mainland: National Income and Economic Development, 1933–1959*. Princeton, N.J.: Princeton University Press.

Articles and Books in Chinese

卜凯：《中国农家经济》，上海：商务印书馆 1937 年版。John Lossing Buck, zhongguo nongjia jingji, Chinese rural economy.

常宗虎：南通现代化：1895–1938》，北京： 中国社会科学出版社 1998 年版。 Chang Zonghu, Nantong Xiandaihua: 1895–1938, The modernization of Nantong: 1895–1938.

陈锋：《也读清初的人丁统计问题》，《平准学刊》 第五辑下册，北京：光明日报出出版社 1989 年版。 Chen Feng, Ye du qingchu de rending tongji wenti, Reassessing the population statistics problem in early Qing dynasty.

陈翰笙、薛暮桥、冯和法编：《解放前的中国农村》，北京： 中国展望出版社 1989 年版。 Chen Hansheng, Xue Muqiao, and Feng Hefa, Jiefang qian de zhongguo nongcun, The Chinese countryside before the liberation.

陈争平：《1895 1936 年中国国际收支与近代化中的资金供给》，《中国经济史研究》 1995 年第4期。 Chen Zhengping, 1895–1936 nian zhongguo guoji shouzhi yu jindaihua zhong de zijin gongji, Chinese international balance of payment and the supply of capital in modernization: 1895–1936, Journal: Zhongguo Jingjishi Yanjiu, Researches in Chinese Economic History.

陈伯庄：平汉沿线农村经济调查》，上海：交通大学研究所 1936 年版。Chen Bozhuang, Pinghan yanxian nongcun jingji diaocha, Investigation of rural economy along Pinghan railroad.

陈正谟：《中国各省的地租》，台北：学海出版社 1971 年版。Chen Zhengmo, Zhongguo gesheng de dizu, Land rent of provinces in China.

从翰香：《近代冀鲁豫乡村》，北京：中国社会科学出版社 1995 年版。Cong Hanxiang, Jindai jiluyu xiangcun, Rural Heibei, Shandong and Henan in modern China.

樊百川：《中国手工业在外国资本主义入侵后的遭遇和命运》，见黄逸平编《中国近代经济史论文选》，上海：上海人民出版社 1985 年版。Fan Baichuan, Zhongguo shougongye zai waiguo zibenzhuyi ruqian hou de zaoyu he mingyun, Chinese handicraft industry's fate after the invasion of foreign capitalism Book: Huang Yiping, Zhongguo Jindai Jingjishi Lunwenxuan, Collected Papers on Modern Chinese Economic History.

方鸿凯和陆炳麟：《民国川沙县志》，上海：上海书店 1991 年版。 Fang Hongkai and Lu Binglin, Minguo chuansha xianzhi, Chuansha County log in Republic of China.

方显廷编：《中国经济研究》，上海：商务印书馆 1939 年版。 Fang Xianting, Zhongguo jingji yanjiu, Research on Chinese economy.

方显廷和毕向辉：《由宝坻手织工业观察工业制度之演变》，《政治经济学报》第四卷第二期，1936 年。 Fang Xianting and Bi Xianghui, You Baodi shouzhigongye guancha gongye zhidu zhi yanbian, The evolution of industry system observed in Baodi's handicraft weaving industry Journal: Zhengzhi Jingjixue Bao, Political Economy Paper.

方显廷：《中国之棉纺织业》，上海：商务印书馆 1934 年版。 Fang Xianting, Zhongguo zhi mianfangzhiye, Cotton weaving industry in China.

方行：《论清代前期棉纺织的社会分工》，《中国经济史研究》 1987 年第 1 期。 Fang Xing, Lun qingdai qianqi mianfangzhi de shehui fengong, On the social division of labor in cotton weaving in early Qing Dynasty. Journal: Zhongguo Jingjishi Yanjiu, Researches in Chinese Economic History.

高王凌：《十八世纪中国的经济发展和政府政策》，北京：中国社会科学出版社 1995 年版。Gao Wangling, Shiba shiji zhonguo de jingji fazhan he zhengfu zhengce, Economic development and governmental policy in China in the 18th century.

顾继瑞：《中国工业史（近代卷）》，南京：江苏科学技术出版社 1992 年版。 Gu Jirui, Zhongguo gongye shi (jindai juan), Chinese industry history (modern volume).

光平：《发展农村手工纺织之研究》，《纺织周刊》 1935 年第五卷第三十一期。 Guang Ping, Fazhan nongcun shougong fangzhi zhi yanjiu, Research on developing handicraft weaving in rural areas. Journal: Fangzhi Zhoukan, Weaving Weekly.

国民政府主计处：《中华民国统计提要：廿四年辑》，上海：商务印书馆 1936 年版。 Republic of China Government Department of Budget, Accounting & Statistics, Zhonghua minguo tongji tiyao: Niansi nian ji Republic of China statistics: the 24th year.

国民政府主计处统计局：《中国租佃制度之统计分析》，重庆：正中书局 1946 年版。 Republic of China Government Department of Budget, Accounting & Statistics, Bureau of Statistics, Zhongguo zudian zhidu zhi tongji fenxi, The statistical analysis of Chinese renting system.

河北省政府建设厅：《调查报告》第四编，第60–61 页，载《中国近代工业史资料》1928 年第三卷。Hebei Province Construction Department, Diaocha baogao vol. 4. Investigation report. In Zhongguo Jindai Gongyeshi Ziliao, Chinese Modern History of Industry Materials.

交通部邮政总局：《中国通邮地方物产志》，上海：商务印书馆 1937 年版。 Ministry of Transportation Bureau of Postal Service, Zhongguo tongyou defang wuchan zhi, Log of products in China where there is postal service.

李伯重：《"男耕女织"与"妇女半边天"角色的形成》，《中国经济史研究》 1997 年第 3 期。 Li Bozhong, Nangeng nvzhi yu funv banbiantian juese de xingcheng, The formation of the division of roles: "man plows while woman weaves" and "women make half the sky". Journal: Zhongguo Jingjishi Yanjiu, Researches in Chinese Economic History.

李伯重：《江南地区的早期工业化》，北京：社会科学文献出版社 2000 年版。 Li Bozhong, Jiangnan diqu de zaoqi gongyehua, Early industrialization in Jiangnan area.

李金铮：《浅谈二三十年代定县的家庭手工棉纺织业》，《河北学刊》 1991 年第 3 期。Li Jinzheng, Qiantan ersanshi niandai dingxian de jiating shougong mianfangzhiye, Brief discussion of family handicraft cotton weaving industry in Ding county in the 20s and 30s Journal: Hebei Xuekan, Hebei Journal of Scholars.

李景汉：《河北省定县农村借贷调查》，《中国农村》1935 年第一卷第六期，载《解放前的中国农村》第三辑。Li Jinghan, Hebeisheng dingxian nongcun jiedai diaocha, Investigation on loans in rural areas of Ding county, Hebei province Journal: Chinese Countryside.

李树青：《清华园附近农村的借贷调查》，清华大学《清华年刊》1933 年第四十卷第十一、十二期，载《解放前的中国农村》第三辑。Li Shuqing, Qinghuayuan fujin nongcun de jiedai diaocha, Investigation on loans in rural areas near Qinghuayuan Journal: Qinghua Journal of Scholars.

李文治:《中国近代农业史资料》，北京：三联书店 1957 年版。Li Wenzhi, Zhongguo jindai nongyeshi ziliao, Chinese modern history of agriculture materials.

李文治：《论明清时代农民经济商品率》，《中国经济史研究》 1993 年第 1 期。Li Wenzhi, Lun mingqing shidai nongmin jingji shangpinly, On rural economy commercial rate in Ming and Qing dynasty Journal: Zhongguo Jingjishi Yanjiu, Researches in Chinese Economic History.

李锡周（编译）:《中国农村经济实况》，北京：北平农民运动研究所出版，1929 年。Li Xizhou, Zhongguo nongcun jingji shikuang, The reality of Chinese rural economy.

厉风:《五十年来商业资本在河北乡村手工业中之发展过程》，《中国农村》 1934 年第一卷第三期。 Li Feng, Wushinian lai shangye ziben zai Hebei xiangcun shougongye zhong zhi fazhan guocheng, The development of commercial capital in rural handicraft industry in Hebei in the recent 50 years Journal: Chinese Countryside.

梁方仲:《中国历代人口、田地、田赋统计》，上海：上海人民出版社 1980 年版。Liang Fangzhong, Zhongguo lidai renkou tiandi tianfu tongji, Statistics of population, land and tax in Chinese dynasties.

林举百:《近代南通土布史》，南通(无正式出版社) 1984 年版。 Lin Jubai, Jindai nantong tubushi, Modern history of homespun in Nantong.

刘克祥和陈争平：《中国近代经济史简编》，杭州：浙江人民出版社 1999 年版。 Liu Kexiang and Chen Zhengping, Zhongguo jindai jingjishi jianbian, Short version of Chinese modern economy history.

罗仑:《明清之际嘉湖地区地主雇工经营的生产力优势》，见洪焕椿和罗仑主编《长江三角洲地区社会 经济史研究》，南京：南京大学出版社 1989 年版。Luo Lun, Mingqing zhi ji jiahu diqu dizhu gugong jingying de shengchanli youshi, The productivity advantage of landlords employing labor in Jiahu area in Ming and Qing dynasties Book: Hong Huanchun and Luo Lun, Changjiang Sanjiaozhou Diqu Shehui Jingjishi Yanjiu, Study of Social and Economic History in Yantze River Delta Area.

潘君祥和王仰清:《上海通史第八卷：民国经济》，上海：上海人民出版社。Pan Junxiang and Wang Yangqing, Shanghai tongshi dibajuan: Minguo jingji, history of Shanghai volume 8: Economy in Republic of China.

彭泽益：《中国近代手工业史资料》第一卷，北京：中华书局 1962a 年版。Peng Zeyi, Zhongguo jindai shougongyeshi ziliao, Chinese modern history of handicraft industry materials.

彭泽益：《中国近代手工业史资料》第二卷，北京：中华书局 1962b 年版。 Peng Zeyi, Zhongguo jindai shougongyeshi ziliao, Chinese modern history of handicraft industry materials.

彭泽益：《中国近代手工业史资料》第三卷，北京：中华书局 1962c 年版。 Peng Zeyi, Zhongguo jindai shougongyeshi ziliao, Chinese modern history of handicraft industry materials.

千家驹：《中国农村经济论文集》，上海：上海书店 1990 年版。Qian Jiaju, Zhongguo nongcun jingji lunwenji, Collected papers on Chinese rural economy.

实业部国际贸易局：《中国实业志：全国实业调查报告》，上海：国际贸易局 1933 年版。Ministry of Industry Bureau of Trade, Zhongguo shiye zhi: Quanguo shiye diaocha baogao, Log of Chinese industry: Report of investigation on nationwide industry.

史建云：《手工业与乡村经济》，见从翰香主编《近代冀鲁豫乡村》，北京：中国社会科学出版社 1995 年版，第 335–439页。 Shi Jianyun, Shougongye yu xiangcun jingji, Handicraft industry and rural economy Book: Cong Hanxiang, Jindai Jiluyu Xiangcun, Rural Heibei, Shandong and Henan in Modern China.

苏征祥：《宝坻县土布》，《商学丛刊》第一期，载 《中国近代手工业史资料》1984 年第二卷。 Su Zhengxiang, Baodixian tubu, Homespun in Baodi county Journal, Shangxue Congkan, Journal Series of Business In Book: Zhongguo Jindai Shougongyeshi Ziliao, Chinese Modern History of Handicraft Industry Materials.

天津档案馆等：《天津商会档案汇编，1903–1911，上卷》，天津：天津人民出版社 1989 年版。Tianjian Archives, Tianjin shanghui dangan huibian 1903–1911 shangjuan, Tianjin association of businessmen archives: 1903–1911, volume I.

王廷元：《论明清时期江南棉纺织业的劳动收益及其经营形态》，《中国经济史研究》 1993 年第 2 期。 Wang Tingyuan, Lun mingqing shiqi Jiangnan mianfangzhiye de laodong shouyi jiqi jingying xingtai, On cotton weaving industry's labor return and its managing model in Jiangnan in Ming and Qing dynasties.

王子建：《中国土布业之前途》，见千家驹编《中国农村经济论文集》，上海：商务印书馆 1935 年版。 Wang Zijian, Zhongguo tubuye zhi qiantu, Future of the Chinese homespun industry, In Book: Qian Jiaju, Zhongguo Nongcun Jingji Lunwenji, Collected Papers on Chinese Rural Economy.

王子建和王镇中：《七省华商生产调查报告》，上海：商务印书馆 1935 年版。Wang Zijian and Wang Zhenzhong, Qisheng huashang shengchan diaocha baogao, Report on investigation on production of Chinese business in seven provinces.

巫宝三：《中国国民所得，1933》，上海：中华书局 1947 年版。Wu Baosan, Zhongguo guomin suode, 1933, National gains of Chinese people, 1933.

吴承明：《我国手工棉纺织业为什么长期停留在家庭手工业阶段》《文史哲》1983 年第 1 期。 Wu Chengming, Woguo shougong mianfangzhiye weishenme changqi tingliu zai jiaing shougongye jieduan, Why cotton weaving industry in our country stagnated in family handicraft stage for a long term Journal: Wenshizhe, Humanities.

吴承明：《资本主义和国内市场》，北京：中国社会科学出版社 1985 年版。Wu Chengming, Zibenzhuyi he guonei shichang, Capitalism and domestic market.

吴馨等：《民国上海县续志》，上海：上海书店 1991 年版。 Wu Xin *et al.*, Minguo shanghaixian xuzhi, Continued log of Shanghai County in Republic of China.

吴知：《关于乡村织布业的一个研究》，上海：商务印书馆 1936 年版。Wu Zhi, Guanyu xiangcun zhibuye de yige yanjiu, A research on rural weaving industry.

吴知：《高阳之土布工业》，载方显廷编《中国经济研究》，1938。Wu Zhi, Gaoyang zhi tubu gongye, Homespun industry in Gaoyang In Book: Fang Xianting, Zhongguo Jingji Yanjiu, Research on Chinese Economy.

萧步才：《江苏省江阴县手工织布业调查资料》，《学术月刊》1958 年第 1 期。 Xiao Bucai, Jiangsusheng jiangyinxian shougongzhibuye diaocha ziliao, Investigation materials on handicraft cotton weaving industry in Jiangyin County, Jiangsu Province Journal: Xueshu Yuekan, Academic Monthly.

徐新吾：《近代中国自然经济加深分解和解体的过程》，《中国经济史研究》1988 年第 1 期。 Xu Xinwu, Jindai zhongguo ziran jingji jiashen fenjie he jieti de guocheng, The process of disintegration of Chinese natural economy in modern China Journal: Zhongguo Jingjishi Yanjiu, Researches in Chinese Economic History.

徐新吾(主编)：《江南土布史》，上海：上海社会科学院出版社 1992 年版。Xu Xinwu (ed), Jiangnan tubu shi, History of homespun in Jiangnan.

许涤新和吴承明（主编）：《中国资本主义的萌芽》，北京：人民出版社 1985 年版。Xu Dixin and Wu Chengming (ed), Zhongguo zibenzhuyi de mengya, The bud of Chinese capitalism.

许涤新和吴承明（主编）：《旧民主主义革命时期的中国资本主义》，北京：人民出版社1990 年版。 Xu Dixin and Wu Chengming (ed), Jiu minzhu zhuyi geming shiqi de zhongguo zibenzhuyi, The Chinese capitalism in old democratic revolution.

许涤新和吴承明（主编）：《新民主主义革命时期的中国资本主义》，北京：人民出版社 1993 年版。 Xu Dixin and Wu Chengming (ed), Xin minzhu zhuyi geming shiqi de zhongguo zibenzhuyi, The Chinese capitalism in neo democratic revolution.

严伟和刘正芬：《民国南汇县续志》，南京：江苏古籍出版社 1991 年版。 Yan Wei and Liu Zhengfen, Minguo nanhuixian xuzhi, Continued log of Nanhui county in Republic of China.

严中平：《中国棉纺织业史稿，1289–1937：从棉纺织工业看中国资本主义发生和发展过程》，北京：科学出版社 1955 年版。 Yan Zhongping, Zhongguo mianfangzhiye shi gao, 1289–1937, Cong mianfangzhiye kan zhongguo zibenzhuyi fasheng he fazhan guocheng, Draft of history of cotton weaving industry in China, 1289–1937, The emergence and development of Chinese capitalism from a perspective of cotton weaving industry.

严中平：《手工棉纺织问题》，《中山文化教育馆季刊》1937 年第四卷第三期，载《中国手工业史资料》。 Yan Zhongping, Shougong mianfangzhi wenti, The question of handicraft cotton weaving, Journal: Zhongshan Wenhua Jiaoyu Guan Jikan, Zhongshan Culture and Education Center Quarterly, In Book: Zhongguo Jindai Shougongyeshi Ziliao, Chinese Modern History of Handicraft Industry Materials.

姚贤镐：《中国对外贸易史资料：1840–1895》，北京：中华书局 1962 年版。Yao Xianhao, Zhongguo duiwai maoyi shi ziliao: 1840–1895, Materials of Chinese foreign trades history: 1840–1895.

于定等：《民国青浦县续志》，南京：江苏古籍出版社 1991 年版。Yu Ding *et al.*, Minguo qingpu xian xuzhi, Continued log of Qingpu county in Republic of China.

张瑞德：《平汉铁路与华北的经济发展，1905–1937》，台北：中央研究院近代史研究所 1986 年版。 Zhang Ruide, Pinghan tielu yu huabei de jingji fazhan, 1905–1937, Pinghan railroad and economic development of Northern China, 1905–1937.

张世文：《定县农村工业调查》，成都：四川民族出版社 1991 年版。 Zhang Shiwen, Dingxian nongcun gongye diaocha, Investigation on rural industry in Ding county.

章有义：《明清及近代农业史论集》，北京：中国农业出版社 1997 年版。Zhang Youyi, Mingqing ji jindai nongye shi lunji, Collected papers on modern agricultural history in Ming and Qing dynasties.

赵冈和陈钟毅：《中国棉业史》，台北：联经出版事业公司 1977 年版。 Zhao Gang and Chen Zhongyi, Zhongguo mianye shi, Chinese history of cotton industry.

中央农业试验所：《农情报告》 1936 年第四卷第十一期。Central agricultural Experimental Institute, Nongqing baogao, Report of agricultural situation.

朱尚英：《高阳布业调查记》，《纺织周刊》 1935 年第五卷第二十三期，载《中国近代手工业史资料》。Zhu Shangying, Gaoyang buye diaocha ji, Gaoyang textile investigation Journal: Fangzhi Zhoukan, Textile Weekly In Book: Zhongguo Jindai Shougongyeshi Ziliao, Chinese Modern History of Handicraft Industry Materials.

Index

CPSIA information can be obtained
at www.ICGtesting.com
Printed in the USA
LVHW050722221218
600626LV00004B/17/P

9 789814 569910